HOW TO
EXPAND
LOVE

His Holiness the
Dalai Lama

HOW TO
EXPAND
LOVE

Widening the Circle
of Loving Relationships

Translated and Edited by
Jeffrey Hopkins, Ph.D.

ATRIA BOOKS
New York London Toronto Sydney

ATRIA BOOKS
1230 Avenue of the Americas
New York, NY 10020

Library of Congress Cataloging-in-Publication Data

Bstan-'dzin-rgya-mtsho, Dalai Lama XIV, 1935–
How to expand love : widening the circle of loving relationships /
His Holiness the Dalai Lama ; translated and edited
by Jeffrey Hopkins.—1st Atria Books hardcover ed.
p. cm.
Includes bibliographical references (p.).
ISBN 0-7432-6968-3 (alk. paper)
1. Love—Religious aspects—Buddhism. 2. Compassion—Religious aspects—
Buddhism. 3. Spiritual life—Buddhism. I. Hopkins, Jeffrey. II. Title.

BQ4570.L6B77 2005
294.3′5677—dc22
2005041022

First Atria Books hardcover edition June 2005

10 9 8 7 6 5 4 3 2 1

ATRIA BOOKS is a trademark of Simon & Schuster, Inc.

Manufactured in the United States of America

For information regarding special discounts for bulk purchases,
please contact Simon & Schuster Special Sales at 1-800-456-6798 or
business@simonandschuster.com.

Contents

Foreword

I met my first teacher of Tibetan Buddhism near the end of 1962 in New Jersey. A Kalmyk Mongolian from Astrakhan, where the Volga River empties into the Caspian Sea, Geshe Wangyal, like many Mongolian monastics, traveled to Tibet to enter a monastic university and stayed there for thirty-five years. Having witnessed the devastation of Buddhist institutions in the Soviet Union, he sensed—after Chinese Communist incursions into Tibet in 1950—what was coming for Tibet, and by 1955 left for India. Three years later he journeyed by ship to the United States with the help of Church World Service.

Almost from the moment of his arrival in the United States, Geshe Wangyal began teaching Tibetan Buddhism to all who sought it, establishing a monastery and learning center and inviting four Tibetan monastics to join him in 1960. They taught many Americans, including myself. Some of these eventually became influential in academics, politics, medicine, religion, publishing, and other fields.

The massive exodus from Tibet in 1959, when the Dalai Lama escaped to India, led to the formation of Tibetan schools for laypersons and monastics in India, Sikkim, and Nepal, including the first monastic education facility in what had been a prison in the heat of Buxaduor, India, a place of painful accommodation to the climate and low altitude of the new environment. Eventually, main monastic institutions of all the major orders of Tibetan Buddhism were reestablished, albeit in diminished form, in India and Nepal. In their new situations, the larger monastic colleges seized the opportunity to reform themselves, dropping certain aspects, such as the institution of the monk-police, the supposed disciplinarians much feared in old Tibet. Other groups created innovative religious educational institutions outside the control of monasteries. Also, lay education on the primary and secondary levels came to include versions of topics hitherto confined to clerics.

Overseas, Tibetan teachers—both monastic and lay— sought to adapt earlier methods of study and practice to more secular environments. At present, after slow but steady success in thousands of centers around the world, we are on the verge of establishing significant centers of Tibetan-style learning outside the Tibetan community. The diaspora has made it possible for parts of Tibet's traditional training dating back more than a thousand years to spread far beyond the land of their origin. Outside Tibet there is a thirst for the rigor of these studies and an appreciation for ancient, time-tested modes of training, even though there are more than considerable difficulties in getting such studies up and running outside their Tibetan and Mongolian environments.

One might think that the world is beset by forces preventing just such a development: increasing tendencies toward exploitation, greed, and lust; rampant consumerism; incessant manipulation of opinions that reinforce coarse urges; the ubiquitous presence of contentless entertainment; increasing divides between rich and poor; sound-bite explanations for complexities of human existence; overeating to the point of pain and obesity; movements to roll back worker rights to nine-teenth-century levels; a ridiculous emphasis on economic profit, as if this could be the only goal of breathing. However, there are signs that these dark forces are producing a backlash of dissatisfaction and a willingness to try other ways.

Many people throughout the world have both a local culture and a global culture, and many have adopted outlooks that have risen to the significance of their original local culture. This openness suggests a readiness for new perspectives, but it could indicate a fractured sense of time, which may threaten the kind of immersion that is required in Tibetan Buddhist practice.

The exiled Tibetan government is moving to embody the democratic principle of separating political control from religious institutions yet still staying within the rubric of Buddhist ideals. This parallels the adaptation of Tibetan educational systems, which have become a mixture of the secular and the religious.

Tibetans living outside their country are struggling to determine what traditional ways to retain—and how to do so. For instance, all of us value the long tradition of Tibetan medicine. The ingenuity of hundreds of physicians over more than a thousand years has resulted in the development of powerful herbal and mineral treatments. As we look at other parts of the world, where modernity has destroyed and replaced old ways of life, and where the wisdom of ancient medical systems has been lost forever, we see the preciousness of the treasure chest of ancient lore preserved in the separate traditions of Tibet and China.

Forests need to be maintained through planned cutting and recultivation to preserve varieties of plants and animals potentially beneficial to the world, but the effort is fraught with problems of displacement and commerce that could condemn people to perpetual poverty; Tibetans too are faced with the conflict between the need to feed people now and market forces that will eventually lay the treasure chest bare. Just as unregulated markets do not make markets free, helter-skelter development does not ensure progress. These are problems the whole world is facing, and there are no easy solutions.

The future well-being of Tibet depends upon the willingness of the Chinese government to set aside its fears and engage in sincere negotiations with the exiled Tibetan government. Is the current Chinese call for negotiations a new tack indicating sincere interest, or is it just another ruse? To this day, the Beijing government has practiced deceit as a delaying tactic, one example being its requirement that Tibet give up the goal of independence, this despite the fact that the Dalai Lama dropped such demands as far back as 1978. The failure of the Chinese government is a lack of love and compassion, which we know from our own lives eventually leads to self-destruction.

Throughout the world love must dissolve intolerance; knowledge must undermine ignorance; coordinated activism must replace passive acceptance and despair; dialogue must replace recrimination; innovative justice must displace vengeance; morality must supplant emphasis on the bottom line; recognition of universal rights must replace disenfranchisement. Only a determined effort over a long period can overcome the entrenched forces of foolishness and greed.

It is my hope that this book on love, in which His Holiness the Dalai Lama draws from a long tradition of Tibetan techniques for transformation of mind and heart, will contribute to what we need so dearly—a sense of love and compassion for each other.

Jeffrey Hopkins, Ph.D.
Professor of Tibetan Studies
University of Virginia

I

My Outlook

If the internal enemy of hatred is not tamed,
When one tries to tame external enemies, they increase.
Therefore, it is a practice of the wise to tame themselves
By means of the forces of love and compassion.

—Bodhisattva Tokmay Sangpo

When I speak about love and compassion, I do so not as a Buddhist, nor as a Tibetan, nor as the Dalai Lama. I do so as one human being speaking with another. I hope that you at this moment will think of yourself as a human being rather than as an American, Asian, European, African, or member of any particular country. These loyalties are secondary. If you and I find common ground as human beings, we will communicate on a basic level. If I say, "I am a monk," or "I am a Buddhist," these are, in comparison to my nature as a human being, temporary. To be human is basic, the foundation from which we all arise. You are born as a human being, and that cannot change until death. All else—whether you are educated or uneducated, young or old, rich or poor—is secondary.

SOLVING PROBLEMS

In big cities, on farms, in remote places, throughout the countryside, people are moving busily. Why? We are all motivated by desire to make ourselves happy. To do so is right. However, we must keep in mind that too much involvement in the superficial aspects of life will not solve our larger problem of discontentment. Love, compassion, and concern for others are real sources of happiness. With these in abundance, you will not be disturbed by even the most uncomfortable circumstances. If you nurse hatred, however, you will not be happy even in the lap of luxury. Thus, if we really want happiness, we must widen the sphere of love. This is both religious thinking and basic common sense.

Anger cannot be overcome by anger. If a person shows anger to you, and you show anger in return, the result is a disaster. In contrast, if you control your anger and show its opposite—love, compassion, tolerance, and patience—then not only will you remain in peace, but the anger of others also will gradually diminish. No one can argue with the fact that in the presence of anger, peace is impossible. Only through kindness and love can peace of mind be achieved.

Only human beings can judge and reason; we understand consequences and think in the long term. It is also true that human beings can develop infinite love, whereas to the best of our knowledge animals can have only limited forms of affection and love. However, when humans become angry, all of this potential is lost. No enemy armed with mere weapons can undo these qualities, but anger can. It is the destroyer.

If you look deeply into such things, the blueprint for our actions can be found within the mind. Self-defeating attitudes arise not of their own accord but out of ignorance. Success, too, is found within ourselves. Out of self-discipline, self-awareness, and clear realization of the defects of anger and the positive effects of kindness will come peace. For instance, at present you may be a person who gets easily irritated. However, with clear understanding and awareness, your irritability can first be undermined, and then replaced. The purpose of this book is to prepare the ground for that understanding from which true love can grow. We need to cultivate the mind.

All religions teach a message of love, compassion, sincerity, and honesty. Each system seeks its own way to improve life for us all. Yet if we put too much emphasis on our own philosophy, religion, or theory, becoming too attached to it, and try to impose it on other people, the result will be trouble. Basically all the great teachers, including Gautama Buddha, Jesus Christ, Muhammad, and Moses, were motivated by a desire to help their fellow beings. They did not seek to gain anything for themselves, nor to create more trouble in the world.

Religion may have become synonymous with deep philosophical issues, but it is love and compassion that lie at the heart of religion. Therefore, in this book I will describe the practice of love that I also do. In experience the practice of love brings peace of mind to myself and helps others. Foolish selfish people are always thinking of themselves, and the result is always negative. Wise persons think of others, helping them as much as they can, and the result is happiness. Love and compassion are beneficial both for you and for others. Through your kindness toward others, your mind and heart will open to peace.

Expanding this inner environment to the larger community around you will bring unity, harmony, and cooperation; expanding peace further still to nations and then to the world will bring mutual trust, mutual respect, sincere communication, and finally successful joint efforts to solve the world's problems. All this is possible. But first we must change ourselves.

Each one of us is responsible for all of humankind. We need to think of each other as true brothers and sisters, and to be concerned with each other's welfare. We must seek to lessen the suffering of others. Rather than working solely to acquire wealth, we need to do something meaningful, something seriously directed toward the welfare of humanity as a whole.

Being motivated by compassion and love, respecting the rights of others—this is real religion. To wear robes and speak about God but think selfishly is not a religious act. On the other hand, a politician or a lawyer with real concern for humankind who takes actions that benefit others is truly practicing religion. The goal must be to serve others, not dominate them. Those who are wise practice love. As the Indian scholar and yogi Nagarjuna says in his *Precious Garland of Advice:*

Having analyzed well
All deeds of body, speech, and mind,

Those who realize what benefit self and others
And always do these are wise.

A religious act is performed out of good motivation with sincere thought for the benefit of others. Religion is here and now in our daily lives. If we lead that life for the benefit of the world, this is the hallmark of a religious life.

This is my simple religion. No need for temples. No need for complicated philosophy. Your own mind, your own heart, is the temple; your philosophy is simple kindness.

2

Stages of Development

Buddhas do not wash away ill deeds with water,
Nor remove sufferings with their hands,
Nor transfer their realizations to others.
Beings are freed through teaching the truth,
the nature of things.

— BUDDHA

In Tibet many great scholar-yogis collected the spiritual practices leading to enlightenment in volumes called *Stages of the Path to Enlightenment.* These eloquent teachings of the compassionate Buddha detail a series of practices that a fortunate person can use for training in order to attain enlightenment. They distill the vast and limitless Buddhist scriptures and commentaries without sacrificing their nature or their essential arrangement. Preserved for the world in Tibet, these precious teachings are wish-fulfilling jewels for fortunate students and trainees.

Stages of the Path to Enlightenment is an instrument for beginners—those who have not previously attained any spiritual heights—telling us which step to take first, and then second, then third, and so on, not confusing what should come before and what should come after. These volumes detail the practices on which we all depend in order to attain enlightenment, gathering in one place the necessary paths first in brief form, and then in extensive form, in accordance with the trainee's ability. This type of presentation is structured for practice that leads to understanding the path.

The practices for beginners come first. When you have practiced those contemplations and received their imprint, your mind becomes capable of deeper topics, and you proceed to the next level. You train in that stage, become proficient, and move on again. It is like schooling; it is not helpful for an infant to enroll in university.

OUTLINE OF THE BOOK

In this book I will present a practical seven-step vehicle for developing love. These techniques are based on the enormous potential of humans to improve, thanks to the fundamental purity of the mind. Thus the book begins with an examination of whether counterproductive emotions are embedded in the fabric of the mind or whether they are peripheral to it and thus capable of being resolved. We conclude that the mind is fundamentally pure, much like the blue sky that exists behind dark clouds. Beginning with this basic vision, we will explore specific instructions for a practice that provides a foundation for the seven key stages of development that follow.

This practice prior to the seven stages deals with overcoming our natural tendency to put others into categories (such as friend or enemy). It reveals how attachment to those categories is based on our assessment of the temporary advantages and disadvantages certain people offer, a misguided approach that restricts such feelings as love and compassion. We will see how our addiction to attractiveness enhances our sympathy for some but undercuts it for others. This initial practice is founded on a sense of equality, our common aspiration to happiness. Meditative exercises on the changeability of situations and relationships are given to help challenge the rigid categories we reflexively apply. A booster technique calls for visualizing two people, one full of praise and the other threatening to attack, in order to learn to recognize and change our knee-jerk responses. The steps in this foundational practice—preliminary meditations, booster techniques, and summary meditations—are like cleaning and sanding a wall before painting a mural of love.

Once equanimity is cultivated, the first step moves to create a strongly positive attitude toward others in ever-widening circles. Exercises begin with choosing your best friend as a model for how to value other not-so-close friends, gradually moving outward to include neutral people, and finally enemies—those who would harm you and your friends. The hardest work here is clearing away the emotional boulders that block progress.

The second step involves practical reflections on the kindness that family and close friends have shown us, especially in childhood, when we are so dependent on the attention and care of others. As we begin to achieve a deeply felt appreciation of kindness, this gratitude can be gradually extended to others beyond our circle of friends. Some exercises in this stage call for remembering kindnesses received over a number of lifetimes; others are aimed at appreciating services provided by others independent of their intention, as in the gift provided by the clerk stocking a shelf in the local supermarket. The booster technique focuses on valuing our enemies because they provide us with unique opportunities to practice patience, tolerance, and forbearance.

The third and fourth steps are correspondent, one strengthening the other. The third calls for reciprocating the kindness of others by developing a heroic intention to further their own enlightenment. This naturally leads to the fourth step, learning to love, which begins with acknowledging how people suffer. We will explore how the cycle of painful situations works, applying this understanding first to ourselves and then extending it to others. At this point, having progressed through the earlier steps that enhance a sense of closeness with others, we can attempt a triad of exercises, gradually increasing in intensity, which expands concern and finally love.

The aim of the exercises up to this point is to become a friend to all beings, to have concern for their situation, and to be ready and able to help. Now the distinction between love and attachment is drawn with more detail. By extending ordinary feelings of love and concern beyond their usual biased limits, love is freed from counterproductive attachment. This process is not a matter of seeking new, otherworldly love, but of using familiar feelings of love and applying them in ever-widening spheres.

The goal is to cultivate in our hearts the concern a dedicated mother feels for her child, and then direct it toward more and more people and living beings. This is heartfelt, powerful love. I will show how these feelings serve a true understanding of human rights, not grounded in legalities or outside dictates but rooted deeply in the heart.

The fifth step is the cultivation of compassion, a deep desire to see others relieved from suffering; this is the other facet of love, a strong wish to see others happy. To be loving and compassionate toward everyone—rich or poor, healthy or sick, young or old—it is crucial to have a consistent sense of their dearness while acknowledging their painful state. The practical exercises in this section create the gradual experience of mercy toward those for whom your feelings are either weak, neutral, nonexistent, or even negative. A booster technique calls for imaginatively switching places with someone obviously suffering from poverty or illness.

The sixth step shows how to become fully committed to altruism, and the seventh and final step turns the experience of unbiased love and compassion toward the highest aim of enlightenment—becoming more effective in helping and serving a wide variety of beings.

Following the stages of the path to enlightenment will transform counterproductive emphasis on yourself into healthy concern for others. By developing your own potential, you can replace self-cherishing with other-cherishing. The multitude of techniques provided for restructuring your relationships in a more even-minded and strongly committed loving framework will ensure that your practice is never dull. Variety will enhance and deepen your experience. Also, certain techniques may be more suited to your disposition and outlook; some methods may be easier and more effective than others.

3

Basic Purity of the Mind

The nature of the mind is clear light.
Defilements are superficial.

—DHARMAKIRTI

Is it possible to get rid of problematic emotions completely, or is it possible only to suppress them? According to a basic Buddhist insight, the mind is essentially luminous and knowing. Therefore, emotional problems do not reside in the mind's essence; such counterproductive attitudes are temporary and superficial, and can be removed.

If distressing emotions such as anger were in the very nature of the mind, then from its inception the mind would always have to be angry. Obviously, this is not so. Only under certain circumstances do we become angry, and when those circumstances are not present, anger is not present either.

What are the circumstances that serve as a basis for generating anger or hatred? When we get angry, the object of our anger appears more awful than what is actually there. You are getting angry because the person has harmed, is harming, or will harm you or your friend. So what is this "I" that is being harmed?

In that flash of rage we feel that both the subject, "I," and the object, the enemy, are solid and independent. Because we accept these appearances as inherently established, anger is generated. However, if at that first flash of rage you make use of reason to ask yourself, Who am I? Who is this one who is being hurt? What is the enemy? Is the enemy the body? Is the enemy the mind? this solidly existing enemy, who previously seemed to be inherently created as something to get angry at, and this "I," who was inherently created to be hurt, seem to disappear. And the anger breaks apart.

Think about it. We get angry at what foils our desires. Anger is fomented by the misconception that the object and yourself are established this way (as enemy and victim) in and of themselves. Hatred is not part of the mind's foundation. It is an attitude without a valid foundation. However, love is validly founded in truth. When, over a long period, an attitude that has a valid foundation competes with an attitude that does not, the one with the valid foundation will overwhelm the other.

Qualities that depend on the mind can be increased limitlessly, and as you increase attitudes that counter distressing emotions, their unfavorable counterparts decrease, finally becoming extinguished altogether. Since the mind has an essential nature of luminosity and knowing, all of us have the fundamental equipment necessary to attain enlightenment.

IDENTIFYING THE MIND

About twenty years ago when I was in Ladakh, India, performing a series of meditations, I had a statue of Shakyamuni Buddha before me, as is still my custom. The gold leaf at the heart of the statue had worn away, and thus that area was brownish in color. As I looked at the heart of the statue, which had no attractive color, watching my mind, eventually thought stopped, and for a short period I felt the luminous and knowing nature of the mind. Subsequently, when I was recollecting this, the experience would return.

It is very helpful in daily practice to identify the nature of the mind and concentrate on it. However, it is hard to catch hold of the mind because it is hidden beneath our own scattered thoughts. As a technique to identify the basic nature of the mind, first stop remembering what happened in the past, then stop thinking about what might happen in the future; let the mind flow of its own accord without the overlay of thought. Let the mind rest in its natural state and observe it for a while.

When, for instance, you hear a noise, between the time of hearing it and conceptualizing its source, you can sense a state of mind devoid of thought but not asleep, in which the object is a reflection of the mind's luminosity and knowing. At such a point the basic nature of the mind can be grasped. In the beginning, when you are not used to this practice, it is quite difficult, but in time the mind appears like clear water. Try to stay with this state of mind without being distracted by conceptual thoughts, and become accustomed to it.

Practice this meditation in the early morning, when your mind has awakened and is clear, but your senses are not yet fully operating. It helps not to have eaten too much the night before, nor to have slept too much; your sleep will be lighter, and this makes the mind lighter and sharper the next morning. If you eat too much, your sleep can be thick and heavy, almost like a corpse. In my own daily routine I eat my fill at breakfast and lunch but just a little bit at night—less than half a cup of crackers; then I go to bed early and rise at three-thirty in the morning to begin meditation.

See if paying attention to the nature of the mind early in the morning makes your mind more alert throughout the day. Your thoughts certainly will be more tranquil. Your memory will improve if you are able to practice a little meditation every day, withdrawing from this scattered mind. The conceptual mind that runs on thinking of good things, bad things, and so forth will get a rest. A little nonconceptuality can provide a much-needed vacation.

Meditation

1. Do not think about what happened in the past or what might happen in the future.

2. Let the mind flow of its own accord without thought.

3. Observe the mind's nature of luminous clarity.

4. Stay with this experience for a while.

You can even practice this while lying in bed in the morning, your mind awake but your senses not yet fully engaged.

COUNTERACTING PROBLEMS

Now let us take a look at counterproductive emotions such as lust, hatred, and jealousy. They all depend upon the initial mistaken belief that objects exist as independent entities, whereas in fact they do not. Through the force of such ignorance, all these other distressing emotions are generated. But as we have seen, when we analyze whether this ignorance and its attendant problems are intrinsic to the nature of the mind itself, we find that, as the Indian scholar-yogi Dharmakirti says, "The nature of the mind is clear light. Defilements are superficial." The nature of the innermost subtle consciousness is pure. Anger, attachment, and so forth are peripheral and do not subsist in the basic mind. We call this the fundamental inborn mind of clear light. Because it makes enlightenment possible, it is also called the Buddha nature. It exists at the root of all consciousness. Also, all of us have some level of compassion, despite differences in development and scope, and all of us have an intelligence that distinguishes between good and bad. These are all conditions for enlightenment.

Once we know that defilements do not dwell in the nature of the mind, it is possible to remove them through generating antidotes to them, attitudes that, like medicine, can counteract them. But if defilements were inseparable from our basic mind, then as long as our mind functioned, bad thoughts—anger and so forth—would have to exist; but this is not the case. At this very instant your mind is reading and thinking; anger is probably not present. Attitudes such as anger and attachment can be separated from the main mind.

At times in our lives, our minds hold on to anger and attachment, and at other times to detachment, contentment, love, and compassion. We cannot feel desire and hatred at exactly the same time toward the very same object. We can certainly have these feelings at different times, but not in the very same moment, which shows that these two attitudes function in contradiction to each other. When one of them increases in strength, the other decreases.

Valid cognition supports love and compassion. Their production needs no assistance from the ignorance that misconceives objects as existing inherently, or in and of themselves alone. Nonvirtuous attitudes such as hatred and pride—no matter how strong they are—are generated only with the assistance and support of ignorance. Therefore, without this misconception of the nature of persons and things, there is no way that desire and hatred can operate. Fortunately, consciousnesses that are the opposites of desire and hatred can operate even when there is no misconception of independent existence.

Ignorance and wisdom both observe the same phenomena, but the ways they perceive them are exactly opposite. Wisdom has a valid foundation, whereas ignorance has no valid foundation and mistakes what it is conceiving. Increasing the strength of wisdom weakens ignorance. Wisdom decreases the misapprehension of the nature of persons and things until ignorance disappears entirely.

THE PROBLEM IS WITHIN

External circumstances are not what draw us into suffering. Suffering is caused and permitted by an untamed mind. The appearance of self-defeating emotions in our minds leads us into faulty actions. The naturally pure mind is covered over by these emotions and troubling conceptions. The force of their deceit pushes us into faulty actions, which leads inevitably to suffering. We need, with great awareness and care, to extinguish these problematic attitudes, the way gathering clouds dissolve back into the sphere of the sky. When our self-defeating attitudes, emotions, and conceptions cease, so will the harmful actions arising from them. As the great late-eleventh- and early-twelfth-century Tibetan yogi Milarepa says, "When arising, arising within space itself; when dissolving, dissolving back into space." We need to become familiar with the state of our own minds to understand how to dissolve ill-founded ideas and impulses back into the deeper sphere of reality. The sky was there before the clouds gathered, and it will be after they have gone. It is also present when the clouds seem to cover every inch of the sky we can see.

The nature of water is not polluted by filth, no matter how dirty. In the same way, the nature of even a troubled mind is not polluted by defilements. The mind of clear light of any being is not polluted even by afflictive emotions like hatred. The next time you feel hatred, see if you can split off from the main run of your mind an observer that watches the hatred. Whereas we usually feel, "I hate . . . ," as if our sense of self and hatred are totally bound up with each other, here you are watching hatred from a slight distance, seeing its faults, which itself naturally causes this excited state to settle down.

To do this, you need first to develop an ability to watch your thoughts, since as long as all of your consciousness is steeped in conceptuality, it is difficult for thought to observe thought. But if, when thoughts arise, you are able to split off an observer that watches them, then gradually you will develop a faculty of consciousness observing consciousness, and even at moments of hatred a factor from within that mind will be able to step outside the anger. By becoming familiar with consciousness as both knower and object known, you can come to recognize what is called "ordinary mind," unaffected by liking and not liking, wanting and not wanting. When the mind is not fractured into many different functions, its natural state of luminosity and knowing can be recognized, and if you stay with this, the experience of luminosity and knowing will increase. Since the inner nature even of hatred is luminous and knowing, hatred will gradually melt into the nature of consciousness.

You do not have to intentionally stop the various thoughts and feelings that dawn in the mind; rather, do not get caught up in them, do not let your mind be drawn into them. The mind will then take on its own natural form, and its clear light nature can be identified. Then its basic purity can be known.

When you understand that clear light is the nature of your inner mind, greater and greater qualities such as love unfold. This is why mental transformation cannot be the result of making changes to your external environment. Acquiring more things once you have what is necessary cannot lead to contentment.

Liberation is attained by knowing the final nature of the mind itself; it is not bestowed on us by someone or something else. Happiness comes through taming the mind; without taming the mind there is no way to be happy. Regardless of the nature of the world, we will not suffer affliction or cause suffering when we trust in the mind's fundamental nature of luminosity, its clear light.

THE DIAMOND MIND

This clear light nature, basic and luminous, is the final root of all minds—forever indestructible, immutable like a diamond. In Buddhism this aspect of the mind is considered permanent in the sense that its continuum is uninterrupted—it has always existed and will go on forever and is therefore not something newly started by causes and conditions.

Our basic mind is essentially pure, naturally devoid of problems from the start. Within it, all pure and impure phenomena appear as manifestations of its spontaneous nature. The unimpeded radiance of the mind is even called compassion, because its effect is compassionate activities, risen out of its essentially pure entity and spontaneous nature.

Pure from the start and endowed with a spontaneous nature, this diamond mind is the basis of all spiritual development. Even while generating a great many good and bad conceptions such as desire, hatred, and bewilderment, the diamond mind itself is free from the corruptions of these defilements, like sky throughout clouds. Water may be extremely dirty, yet its nature remains clear. Similarly, no matter what afflictive emotions are generated as the artifice of this diamond mind, and no matter how powerful they are, the basic mind itself remains unaffected by defilement; it is good without beginning or end.

Wonderful spiritual qualities, such as unbounded love and compassion, are all present in basic form in this diamond mind; their manifestation is prevented only by certain temporary conditions. In a sense we are enlightened from the very beginning, endowed with a completely good basic mind.

VALUING THE PRESENT SITUATION

By being born a human, you have taken on a physical support system through which you can easily achieve both your temporary and your larger aims. Now that you have attained this auspicious life form so unique among the myriad forms born into this world, it is important that you do not waste it. If in this situation you practice merely to attain a good life in future rebirths for yourself, you would not be using your potential fully. Or, if you merely aim to liberate yourself from the tangles of suffering, this would also fall short of your inherent potential. With your humanity you should do whatever you can to attain perfect, complete spiritual development.

Meditation

1. Reflect on the potential of your current situation for spiritual growth: you have a human body; spiritual teachings are available in your environment;

you have the mental capacity to internalize spiritual teachings—you have pure diamond mind.

2. Value the current opportunity for spiritual practice.

3. Set as your motivation a wish to help not only yourself but all beings.

4. Aim to help others.

4

Foundational Step: Viewing Friend and Foe

At present you find it unbearable that your friends suffer, but you are pleased that your enemies suffer, and you are indifferent to the suffering of neutral persons.

—TSONGKHAPA, *GREAT TREATISE ON THE STAGES OF THE PATH*

Out of the foundation of the mind's true nature, you need to develop love and compassion so strong that the suffering of others becomes unbearable. Since love and compassion must be felt equally for all beings of all types, the strength of these attitudes will depend upon the degree of closeness and dearness that you feel for others. For instance, when an intimate friend falls ill, your sense of love and compassion, your wish that this person be freed from sickness and restored to health, is stronger than it might be for a mere acquaintance, or for someone whom you do not like. This type of love and compassion is mixed with desire to pursue some benefit for yourself.

If a formerly attractive person with a pleasant personality loses his or her good looks or character, your readiness to sympathize with that person might disappear. If you have a sense of compassion for an ugly person, then no matter how that person's appearance changes, the sense of compassion is not lost. In the first example compassion is mixed with desire: the person has attracted you. Your mind has exaggerated the pleasant features of that person so that desire is generated, and you feel a longing, a mixture of intimacy and wishing to lessen whatever suffering he or she is undergoing. However, pure compassion is not biased or partial; it is thoroughly imbued with equanimity and encompasses both friend and foe.

Without a sense of equality, unbiased love and compassion cannot even get started. Once you have generated an attitude of equality toward all, then it will be possible to view not just friends but neutral beings and even enemies with great endearment. This is not easy. It is difficult to develop a sense of closeness to everyone. Reflective meditation is needed.

EQUALITY

Begin by noting that within our minds we have three main categories for people—friends, neutral beings, and enemies. We may have many attitudes toward them, but three are our concern here—lust, indifference arising from neglect, and hatred, respectively. When any of these three attitudes is present, it is impossible to generate a sense of closeness with everyone. Lust, hatred, and indifference must be neutralized.

Meditation

Here is how we can cultivate equanimity in meditation.

1. Simultaneously visualize a friend, an enemy, and a neutral person.

2. Examine your feelings to see who is being held closely and who is being considered at a distance. You feel naturally close to your friend; regarding your enemy, you feel not only distant but sometimes also anger or irritation; you feel nothing for the neutral person. Investigate why.

3. Consider whether the friend appears to be close because she has helped you or your friends.

4. Consider whether the enemy appears to be distant because he has harmed you or your friends.

5. Consider whether you feel indifference toward the neutral person because she has neither helped nor harmed you or your friends.

6. Realize that, like yourself, all of these people want happiness and do not want pain, and in this important way they are equal.

7. Remain with this realization until it sinks into the depths of your mind.

ENHANCEMENT

If you are open to the possibility that past and future rebirth over a continuum of lives may take place, you could enhance the perception of equality by considering the implications of rebirth. A continuum of lives means our births are beginningless. Over the course of many lifetimes everyone has likely been in many types of relationships with everyone else. You cannot be sure that those who are now your friends were always friends in the past and that those who are now your enemies were always your enemies. Even in this one lifetime, there are persons who early on were enemies but later turned into friends, and others who were friends but later became enemies. Looking toward the future, there is no reason why an enemy must remain an enemy and a friend remain a friend. Friends, enemies, and neutral people are equal because they may shift interchangeably from one role to the next.

Consequently, there is no way to completely decide finally that a certain person is forever your enemy and therefore should be discarded, or that someone else is forever your friend and therefore should be cherished, or that someone will always be a neutral person and therefore should be treated with indifference. Rather, all have acted equally as enemy, friend, and neutral party. If someone harmed you last year but helped you this year, and another person helped you last year but harmed you this year, they would be equal, would they not? This is why there is no sense in single-pointedly considering a certain person to be just a friend and another person to be just an enemy, or just neutral. Our basic life structure is not at all stable: sometimes we are successful, sometimes unsuccessful. Things are always changing, changing, changing. That we experience such solid and stable feelings toward friends and enemies is simply wrong. There is no reason to assume such rigidity; it is foolish. Reflecting on this will gradually bring your mind to equanimity.

Meditation

1. Consider that even during the span of this lifetime, there is no certainty that specific individuals will always be friends, enemies, or neutral. Consider examples of this from your own life—a neutral person who became a friend; a neutral person who became an enemy; a friend who became neutral, or an enemy; an enemy who became a friend.

2. Visualize someone who is presently a neutral being and imagine that she brought help and harm in past lifetimes.

3. Imagine that a friend who has helped a lot in this lifetime brought harm to you in a previous lifetime and was neutral at other times.

4. Imagine that an enemy who has harmed you in this lifetime was neutral in some other life and brought repeated benefits in another.

5. See that in the longer perspective of many lifetimes, friend, enemy, and neutral observer have all equally helped and harmed you or your friends, so it cannot be concluded that they are solely one way or the other.

6. Realize that in terms of the long course of beginningless rebirth, none of us could decide that someone who has helped or harmed us in this life has been doing so for all lifetimes.

7. Decide that it is not right to single out one for intimacy, another for neutral indifference, and yet another for alienation.

Reflecting this way, deepen your sense of equal feeling toward friends, enemies, and neutral persons.

It might seem more crucial to consider what others are doing for you or to you in the present rather than several lifetimes ago, but this is not so. As we have shown, a person's status as friend or foe can change even in one lifetime. Help or harm from another is temporary, and mere timing cannot be the basis for choosing intimacy or alienation. Decide that it is impractical to single-mindedly desire those presently helping you and to single-mindedly hate those who are presently harming you.

BOOSTER TECHNIQUE

When you contemplate this matter, the single-minded apprehension of some people as friends and others as enemies, and the consequent generation of desire and hatred, will become weaker in strength. Still, to bring the implications of these meditations home, it is helpful to reflect on a more dramatic scene.

1. Visualize two persons.

2. Imagine that one of them is brandishing a fist at you.

3. Reflect on the reason for becoming uncomfortable: you seem to be in imminent danger of being struck.

4. Vividly imagine that the other person is at the same time doing something pleasant for you—

praising you, giving you a present, or stroking your arm.

5. Examine why you are so pleased with this. It is due to a minor temporary circumstance that you are so pleased.

6. Understanding this, consider that your reactions with regard to friends and enemies are not very profound.

CONCLUDING MEDITATION

There is no certainty that a friend, an enemy, or a neutral person will at all times either help, harm, or do neither. When negative thoughts and motivations such as hatred or anger are present, even a friend is seen as an enemy, but when negative thoughts toward an enemy disappear, the enemy becomes a friend. Reflect on the following:

1. From their own point of view friends, enemies, and neutral beings equally want happiness and do not want suffering.

2. From your own point of view each and every one of them has been your friend limitless times over beginningless cyclic existence and will definitely help you again in the future; each has been your enemy just as often; and each has equally been neutral.

3. Thus from whatever side it is considered, your own or others', there is no point in exaggerated conceptions of intimacy and alienation. You should not value one person as basically good and another as bad, even though his present actions may be good or bad, helpful or harmful. There is no reason to be nice to one person and not nice to another. Though it is true that persons temporarily are friends or enemies—helpful or harmful—it is incorrect to single anyone out for attraction or hatred.

It is important to perform these reflective meditations with specific people in mind and not just directed at all sentient beings, the latter being too vague to effect a real change of attitude. By working on individuals, slowly extending this feeling out toward more and more people, you will develop a sense of equanimity toward the whole of the living world.

Through this meditation, you eventually arrive at a point where generating strong feelings of desire or hatred appears to be senseless. Bias weakens, and you decide that rigidly classifying people as friends and enemies has been a mistake.

Like smoothing a wall before painting a mural or preparing a field before planting, the cultivation of a true feeling of equality provides the groundwork for the next step in the path to love: recognizing all sentient beings as the best of friends. Now the cultivation of equality will serve as the foundation for love.

5

The First Step: Recognizing Friends

While you see that those close to you are
drowning in the ocean of cyclic existence,
And are as if fallen into a whirlwind of fire,
There is nothing more awful than to work for
your own liberation,
Neglecting those whom you do not
recognize due to the process of death and rebirth.

—CHANDRAGOMIN, *LETTER TO A STUDENT*

Having created an equal attitude toward friends, enemies, and neutral persons, you have a foundation for viewing every being as your closest friend. The aim now is to develop a true feeling of intimacy with everyone. Since endearment is generated easily for friends, you need a technique for cultivating the recognition of all beings as friends, using your own best friendships as the model. Who is your best friend?

Another approach is to use your mother's unconditional love as a model. Because I was identified as the reincarnation of the Thirteenth Dalai Lama, I did not live at home after the age of three or four. As a child I visited my mother practically every day, or she would come to see me, since my family lived near my residence in Lhasa, the capital of Tibet. She always had a good heart, very compassionate, caring a great deal about others who were needy. She was kind to everyone. She never scolded me, although later she told me that I would get upset when I did not get my way, and I would yank at her earring when she was carrying me. She said that one day I pulled so hard, it wounded her earlobe.

From the time I was four, the person who gave me food every day in Lhasa was a bald, bearded fellow named Ponpo. I was very close to him; he was like a mother. When I was at the Summer Palace memorizing religious texts, he always had to be near; I would cry if he was not. I had to at least see the bottom of his robe while he sat on the other side of a screen a few feet from the door. He had to stay there; otherwise, I would cry. Ponpo, who had been the cook for the previous Dalai Lama, did not know how to tell stories, did not know how to play, and was not educated in terms of either religion or other topics. I valued him so much because he fed me and took care of me.

It seems to me that we, like other mammals such as dogs and cats, cherish most those who feed us. We love our mothers not because they gave birth to us but because they gave us milk and took care of us. When I was sick, Ponpo would carry me around or hold me on his lap. When you hold a kitten on your lap, the kitten will purr; it is the same with children. I liked him a lot.

Everyone, whether religious or not, can understand from natural experience and common sense that affection is really important from the day of birth; it is the basis of life. The very survival of our body requires the affection of others, to which we also respond with affection. Though it is mixed with attachment, this affection is not based on physical or sexual attraction. This kind of affection, though not unbiased, can be expanded to cover all sentient beings, making it unbiased. This is what it means to expand love.

For the following meditation, if your relationship with your mother is complicated, you can consider ideal motherhood instead, or you can use any intimate, friend, or family member.

Meditation

First, let us consider the underpinnings of this meditation. The format is built on the assumption of rebirth, which if you have an inkling might be true, you can use to probe the implications of beginningless rebirth for your relations with others. However, if you do not suspect that rebirth is true, it is still possible to utilize these steps as a purely imaginative exercise to help undo knots in your relationships.

1. Reflect that if there is rebirth, cyclic existence means that your own births have had no beginning.

2. Consider that when you were born from a womb as an animal or a human, or from an egg as a bird, a fish, or a spider, you required a mother. And because your births are innumerable, you must have had innumerable mothers over your many lifetimes. The implication is that every living being has been your mother at some time. If you have trouble coming to that conclusion, see if you can follow the continuum of lifetimes and discover any sentient being who has not been your mother; such a conclusion is impossible.

3. Observe that the times you were born from a womb or an egg are unlimited, and therefore your mothers are also unlimited.

4. Reflecting on these points, understand that each sentient being in your present life was your mother many times. Do not rush through these steps; the aim here is not to accept superficial logic, but to imbue your mind and attitudes with the impact of the perspective of rebirth. Try it on, so to speak, and see if it is helpful.

   • Think of your best friend and identify that this friend was, at some time over the continuum of lives, a nurturing friend. Keep this person in mind until you feel a change of perspective.

   • Then gradually consider other, not so close, friends one by one in the same way, identifying and feeling that over the continuum of lives, they were very close to you. It can take many days to do this—even weeks.

   • Then bring to mind a neutral person—someone who has neither helped nor harmed you in this lifetime. Consider that this person also over the continuum of lives was at certain times as close and as nurturing as your closest friend.

- Gradually extend this realization to other neutral persons—those seen on a subway, passed on the street, or seen in a store.

- When you become somewhat proficient at identifying friends and neutral persons who have nurtured you, and can feel how your perspective changes, consider someone who has harmed you or your friends a little. Start with a minor enemy, such as a person who said something critical about you, so that you can develop experience with temporarily setting aside negative feelings in favor of realizing that at some time you were close friends. If you jump too soon into considering people whom you strongly dislike, your negative opinions will likely halt your progress.

- When you feel your perspective change toward that minor enemy, stay with that new attitude for a while, then slowly consider the next level of enemy.

Through practice it is possible to perceive every sentient being as a friend. Easy to say, but hard to do. Do not become discouraged; keep performing these steps over and over again. Gradually accumulate experience.

For me, since I carry the responsibility for the welfare of Tibet, the most difficult people to perceive as friends are those who are deliberately harming the Tibetan people. Still, from experience with friends, neutral persons, and lesser enemies, I can see that they are basically no different.

What keeps me from being discouraged despite more than fifty years of working for Tibet without much success is first that the cause is just, true, honest, and helpful to others. That a cause is true is not sufficient; it must be beneficial. My work for Tibet does not increase either my fame, influence, power, or profit in any way; it is for the Tibetan people, who have a right to be free and to preserve Buddhist teachings helpful to all sentient beings. Thus whether we achieve our goal in our own lifetime or not, it is worthwhile to maintain the struggle. We are at a critical point due to the rapid influx of Chinese into Tibet; like Manchuria and Inner Mongolia, which have become completely assimilated into Chinese culture, Tibetan culture may disappear if the current trend continues. A hopeful sign is that nowadays people of the world, including many Chinese themselves, are more conscious of what is happening—the possible loss to the world of a valuable culture—and thus there is more moral concern. The cause will continue from generation to generation; unlike a political term of office, it is not limited by a certain demarcation of time. These are my reasons for staying enthusiastic.

BOOSTER TECHNIQUE

Between meditations, occasionally identify whomever you encounter as having been a nurturing friend. For instance, when passing a neutral person in a crowd, think: This person does not seem to have any relation to me in this lifetime, but over the continuum of lives has definitely been my mother, father, child, or closest friend. In this way you will slowly develop the feeling that all sentient beings are your friends.

MEASURE OF SUCCESS

With much practice comes conditioning: even when you see a bug, you will think, Oh, this being has been born in such a stricken condition! Even though I am human, and this being is a bug, in the past she was my mother, and I was her child. At that time my life depended on her, and she cherished me more than her own life. After sufficient meditation, this type of thought will arise spontaneously. The sign of having successfully completed your recognition of all sentient beings as nurturing friends is when you look at the world around you and think, Beings from animals on up took care of me in former lifetimes not just once but many times.

6

The Second Step: Appreciating Kindness

When you were hungry and thirsty, she gave you food and drink; when you were cold, clothes; when you had nothing, she gave you everything of value.

—TSONGKHAPA, *GREAT TREATISE ON THE STAGES OF THE PATH*

Governments now use sophisticated technology to track possible troublemakers, but terrorists still succeed. No matter how sophisticated technology becomes, the opposing side will respond. The only effective defense is internal. This may sound naive, but the only way to stop terror is through altruism. Altruism means having a basic concern for and appreciation of others, which comes from realizing their kindnesses to you.

In this second step you reflect on the kindness that others individually afforded to you when, over the course of lifetimes, they were your parents and you were a child.

Applying this reflection to each encounter, you will see that all beings have equally shown kindness to you either in this lifetime or in others.

Meditation

In the previous step you visualized and recognized others as close friends, and now it is possible to become mindful of their kindness when they were your best friends. Again, it may be easiest to begin with your own mother in this lifetime, since she most likely was your primary nurturer. But if she was not, or if your relationship is complicated, use whoever is the most nurturing person in your life as the model for reflection, converting the following meditation as appropriate:

1. Visualize your mother, or prime nurturer, vividly in front of you.

2. Think:

   This person was my mother many times over the continuum of lives. Even in just this lifetime, she has bestowed on me a body that supports an auspicious life through which I am able to progress spiritually. She sustained me in her womb for nine months, during which she could not behave as she wished but had to pay special attention to this burden that she carried in her body, making it heavy and difficult to move about. Even though my movements would cause her pain, she would take delight in them, thinking how strong her child was, rather than becoming angry and concentrating on her pain. Her sense of closeness and dearness was great.

Stay a while with this thought, feeling its impact.

3. Deepen your appreciation by considering details: While giving birth, she suffered greatly, and afterward she was constantly concerned with my welfare, wondering how I was doing, valuing the child born from her own body higher than anything else. Later, she sustained me in the very best way she could.

   She wiped away my feces and removed mucus from my nose. She gave her own milk and did not take offense when I bit her nipples. Even when she was bothered by such things, her sense of endearment for me was utmost in her mind. This was not just for a day, a week, a month, but from year to year, whereas for most people taking care of a child for an hour or two is bothersome.

If you are using as your model a person other than your mother, recall in detail these kindnesses he or she extended to you.

4. Realize how dependent you were:

> If she had abandoned me for even an hour or two, I could have died. Through her kindness in sustaining me with the best of food and clothing according to her ability, this precious life with a physical body that makes spiritual progress possible was maintained.

Appreciate the kindness you received. When you carefully consider her kindness in these ways, there is no way to be unimpressed.

5. Increase the scope of your appreciation to other lifetimes:

> She was kind not only during this life but also in other lifetimes as a human or as an animal,

since most animals care for their young in similar ways.

Let the impact of this new perspective sink in, and do not rush on to the next phase as if this were just a superficial exercise.

6. Having understood the kindness of your prime nurturer in this lifetime, extend this felt understanding gradually to other friends. Think about how when they were your mother or best of friends, they protected you with great kindness, just as your prime nurturer has done. Reflect slowly and carefully about their kindness, starting with your next closest friend and considering, as you did above:

This person was my mother many times over the continuum of lives. Even in just this lifetime, she has bestowed on me a body that supports an auspicious life through which I am able to progress spiritually. She sustained me in her womb for nine months, during which she could not behave as she wished but had to pay special attention to this burden that she carried in her body, making it heavy and difficult to move about. Even though my movements would cause her pain, she would take delight in them, thinking how strong her child was, rather than becoming angry and concentrating on her pain. Her sense of closeness and dearness was great.

Stay a while with this thought, feeling its impact. Then, deepen your appreciation by considering details:

While giving birth, she suffered greatly, and afterward she was constantly concerned with my welfare, wondering how I was doing, valuing the child born from her own body higher than anything else. Later, she sustained me in the very best way she could.

She wiped away my feces and removed mucus from my nose. She gave her own milk and did not take offense when I bit her nipples. Even when she was bothered by such things, her sense of endearment for me was utmost in her mind. This was not just for a day, a week, a month, but from year to year, whereas for most people taking care of a child for an hour or two is bothersome.

Realize how dependent you were, appreciating the person's kindness when she or he was your mother or prime nurturer:

> If she had abandoned me for even an hour or two, I could have died. Through her kindness in sustaining me with the best of food and clothing according to her ability, this precious life with a physical body that makes spiritual progress possible was maintained.

Feel the impact of viewing this person as having been kind in these ways. Then increase the scope of your appreciation to other lifetimes:

> This is true not only during this life but also in other lifetimes as a human and as an animal, since most animals care for their young in similar ways.

Stay with these feelings, and appreciate the positive enhancement of your attitude toward that person.

7. When the force of this reflection has been felt, pass to the next friend, meditating in the same manner, slowly considering all your friends.

Neutral Beings

Then consider a neutral being, someone who has neither helped nor harmed you in this lifetime—even someone you saw in a photograph about whom you know little or nothing—in the same way (begin with number 6, on page 55). When you have done so, stay with this changed perspective, allowing these warm feelings to grow. Then, one by one consider other neutral beings until your positive attitude embraces all of them.

Enemies

Now you have reached the most difficult part. Having become accustomed to considering friends and neutral persons this way, you are ready to reflect on persons who have intentionally or unintentionally harmed you and your friends in this lifetime. With friends and neutral persons, you know how it feels to change your perspective in a more positive direction, which makes it easier for you to make sure your meditation does not become just words, now that you are considering those who have harmed you.

Visualize an enemy clearly in front of you; feel the presence of this person and think:

First: This person was my mother many times over the continuum of lives. Even in just this lifetime, she has bestowed on me a body that supports an auspicious life through which I am able to progress spiritually. She sustained me in her womb for nine months, during which she could not behave as she wished but had to pay special attention to this burden that she carried in her body, making it heavy and difficult to move about. Even though my movements would cause her pain, she would take delight in them, thinking how strong her child was, rather than becoming angry and concentrating on her pain. Her sense of closeness and dearness was great.

Second: While giving birth, she suffered greatly, and afterward she was constantly concerned with my welfare, wondering how I was doing, valuing the child born from her own body higher than anything else. Later, she sustained me in the very best way she could.

She wiped away my feces and removed mucus from my nose. She gave her own milk and did not take offense when I bit her nipples. Even when she was bothered by such things, her sense of endearment for me was utmost in her mind. This was not just for a day, a week, a month, but from year to year, whereas for most people taking care of a child for an hour or two is bothersome.

Third: If she had abandoned me for even an hour or two, I could have died. Through her kindness in sustaining me with the best of food and clothing according to her ability, this precious life with a physical body that makes spiritual progress possible was maintained.

Fourth: This is true not only during this life but also in other lifetimes as a human or as an animal, since most animals care for their young in similar ways.

Conclusion: Therefore, although this person has appeared to me in this lifetime as an enemy seeking harm to my body and spirit, in former lifetimes she was my best friend, my mother, sacrificing her own body and spirit for me. The times she did this are innumerable.

By meditating in this manner, it is possible to identify even an enemy as having at some time been your nourisher and having been extremely kind. Extend this felt understanding to other enemies one by one in the same way. Consider each person for as long as it takes until your feeling is the same as it is for your closest nurturer. Since it makes no difference whether a person has been kind to you recently or a while ago, decide that all beings have been equally kind to you over the course of many lifetimes.

Such reorientation of your relationships with others gives your life new meaning. Meditating this way is worthy of lifelong endeavor. Eventually, what you have meditated will arise spontaneously.

BOOSTER TECHNIQUE: BECOMING AWARE OF UNINTENDED KINDNESS

To deepen your gratitude toward all people, it is helpful to reflect on the unintended kindness of those who provide goods and services without necessarily knowing the names or faces of those whom they serve. We live in dependence upon those who have no special motivation to help us.

When we want rain and it rains, we are grateful even

though there is no motivation on the part of the shower to help us. Also, if we want a grove of trees to roam in, we are happy to have that grove and value it even though the stand of trees itself has no motivation to help. Similarly, sentient beings provide necessities for your life; they are helping you in particular without ever knowing you in particular. In this life there are so many facilities we enjoy—nice buildings, roads, and so forth—that are produced by other people. As you can see, thousands of people in this lifetime, whom you may never meet, are showing you kindness.

Here are some sample contemplations:

1. Think of all the food in a supermarket and all the persons involved in making it available—from the farmers to the truckers to the persons who put it on the shelves.

2. Realize that even a glass of water depends on a vast nexus of individuals.

3. Contemplate that all the facilities we use—buildings, roads, and so forth—are produced by other people.

Providing services is a form of kindness, of nurturing, no matter what the motivation may be. When you experience this nexus of kindness in a deep way, it becomes possible to extend this appreciation even to your enemies.

Including Enemies

Most of our good qualities are produced in conjunction with other people. As I will explain in the final chapter, the practice of virtues like giving depends almost entirely on other sentient beings. Similarly, choosing to abandon harmful actions like killing and stealing is mostly done in relation to other sentient beings.

The worst consequence of not being mindful of the unintended kindness of others comes into view when we consider our enemies. Without enemies you could not fully engage in the practice of patience—tolerance and forbearance. We need enemies, and should be grateful to them. From the viewpoint of training in altruism, an enemy is really your guru, your teacher; only an enemy can teach you tolerance. An enemy is the greatest teacher of altruism, and for that reason, instead of hating, we must respect him.

We have learned that it is not necessary for someone

to have a good motivation toward you in order for you to respect and cherish that person. For example, we seek the alleviation of suffering, and even though the alleviation of suffering itself does not have any motivation at all, we cherish, value, and respect it highly. The presence or absence of motivation makes no difference in terms of whether something or someone can be helpful in accumulating positive forces for shaping the future, what Buddhists call "merit." It is only in relation to those wishing us harm—enemies—that we can truly cultivate the highly meritorious virtue of patience. Thus an enemy is absolutely necessary. Without patience, you could not develop true love and compassion because you would be subject to irritation.

True love and compassion extends even to those whose motivation is to harm you. Try to imagine that enemies purposefully get angry in order to help you accumulate merit. If your life goes along too easily, you become soft. Tragic circumstances help you develop inner strength, the courage to face them without emotional breakdown. Who teaches this? Not your friend, but your enemy.

Meditation

Here is how to widen the circle of appreciation to include enemies:

1. Consider that in order for you to become enlightened, the practice of patience is essential.

2. See that in order to practice patience, you need an enemy.

3. Understand that in this way enemies are very valuable for the opportunities they provide.

4. Decide that instead of getting angry at those who block your wishes, you will inwardly respond with gratitude.

This is very difficult but very rewarding. Consider the matter deeply, and you will see that even great enemies who intend you harm are also extending great kindness to you. Only when faced with the work of enemies can you learn real inner strength.

In my own life, the most difficult periods have been the times of greatest gain in knowledge and experience.

Through a difficult period you can learn to develop inner strength, determination, and courage to face the problem. If you become discouraged, that is the real failure; you have lost a valuable chance to develop. To remain determined is itself a gain. During a difficult period you can come closer to reality, to peeling off all pretensions. When things go smoothly, life can easily become like an official ceremony in which protocol, like how you walk and how you speak, is more important than content. But at a time of crisis these things are pointless—you have to deal with reality and become more practical.

Enemies give us this kind of chance. Also, when you think in terms of the practice of patience, an enemy is the most benevolent of helpers. Through cultivating patience your merit increases; thus, enemies are the main instigators of spiritual advancement.

LEARNING FROM TRAGEDY

If you see that some situation or person is going to cause you suffering, it is important to engage in techniques to avoid it; but once suffering has started, it should be received not as a burden but as something that can assist you. Undergoing small sufferings in this lifetime can purify the karma of many ill deeds accumulated in former lifetimes. Adopting this perspective will help you see the ills of cyclic existence, and the more you can do this, the more you will dislike engaging in nonvirtues. Hardship also helps you to see the advantages of liberation. In addition, through your own experience of suffering, you will be able to empathize with the pain of others and generate a wish to do something for them. So, seen in this way, suffering can provide a remarkable opportunity for more practice and more thought.

From this viewpoint, enemies are teachers of inner strength, courage, and determination. This does not mean you should give in to those who would harm you. Depending on the enemy's attitude, you may have to defend yourself strongly, but deep down try to maintain your calm by realizing that, like you, she is a person who wants happiness and does not want suffering. It is hard to believe, but over time, it is possible to develop such an attitude. Here is how to do it:

Consider the so-called enemy. Because this person's mind is untamed, she engages in activities to bring injury to you. If anger—the wish to harm—were in the very nature of this person, it could not be altered in any way, but as we have seen, hatred does not subsist in the nature of a person. And even if it were the nature of a person to hate, then just as we cannot get angry at fire because it burns our hand (it is the very nature of fire to burn), so should we not get angry at a person expressing her nature. This said, hatred actually is peripheral to a person's nature. Thus, just as when a cloud covers the sun, we do not get angry at the sun, so we should not get angry at the so-called enemy, but instead hold the person's afflictive emotion responsible.

We ourselves sometimes engage in bad behavior, do we not? Still, most of us do not think we are completely bad. We should look on others the same way. The actual troublemaker is not the person, but his or her afflictive emotion.

When we lose our temper, we have no hesitation about speaking harsh words even to a close friend. Afterward, when we cool down, we feel embarrassed about what happened. This indicates that we, as persons, do not want to use such harsh words, but because we lost our power, and were dominated by anger, something happened outside our control. One day my driver in Tibet was working under my car and bumped his head against the chassis; he got so angry, he hit his head against the car a couple of times as if to punish the vehicle, but of course he hurt himself instead.

As I mentioned earlier, we can learn to separate a corner of the mind from strong emotions like hatred and watch it; this indicates that the mind and hatred are not one; the person and hatred are not one.

IMPACT OF SUCCESSFUL MEDITATION

When through meditation you gain more appreciation both for the motivated kindnesses bestowed on you by friends, enemies, and neutral beings over the course of lifetimes and for the unintended kindnesses of those essential provisions you depend on daily, you will contribute to a healthier society. Without the appreciation of kindness, society breaks down. Human society exists because it is impossible to live in complete isolation. We are interdependent by nature, and since we must live together, we should do so with a positive attitude of concern for one another. The aim of human society must be the compassionate betterment of all from one lifetime to the next.

As small children we very much depend on the kindness of our parents. Again in old age we depend on the kindness of others. Between childhood and old age we falsely believe we are independent, but this is not so.

7

The Third Step:
Returning Kindness

Kindness unrepaid weighs more heavily
Than a great mountain or the ocean.

—TSONGKHAPA, *GREAT TREATISE ON THE STAGES OF THE PATH*

When you have thoroughly contemplated the previous steps, recognizing all beings as friends and nurturers through a continuum of lives and appreciating their intentional and unintentional kindnesses, you will indeed feel that you *must* return their kindness. But how can you help them? No matter what type of prosperity you might be able to bring them within the round of birth, aging, sickness, and death, it would be temporary and superficial. The deepest help would be to lead them to true happiness, the ultimate aim of lifetime after lifetime. Providing opportunities for others to improve their living condition affords temporary and necessary help, but by teaching others specific practices of mind, and heart, and body, it is possible to lead them to enlightenment. The greatest reciprocation of the kindness of others is liberation from all types of suffering.

Meditation

1. Consider this:

   My mother (or best friend) in this lifetime is blind and not in the best frame of mind. She is walking along the edge of a frightful cliff without a guide; it would be awful if I, her own child, did not pay attention and take on the task of helping her.

2. Extend the example:

   All sentient beings throughout space and time have been my mother, protecting me with great kindness; they do not know what to let go and what to adopt in their behavior in order to create their own happiness. With no spiritual guide, they are walking along the edge of a cliff of frightful suffering within cyclic existence. It would be awful to know that each step brought them closer to misery, and I did not consider their welfare but only my own freedom.

Stay a while with your perception of their perilous situation, feeling its impact. Allow yourself to care about everyone's situation. If this seems vague, reflect on particular beings in such a horrible situation, and then extend your intense feeling to everyone. Success cultivating the earlier steps with regard to individual beings makes this possible.

3. Commit yourself to the welfare of others. Just as they have taken care of you in this and other lifetimes as close friends, or by providing you with essential services, be determined to help them in whatever way is appropriate:

    I will do whatever I can for these beings—my own nurturing friends—stricken by such suffering.

4. Imagine offering various forms of happiness to living beings.

In time, a heartfelt sense of reciprocation will become your first feeling toward others, and the bedrock of your relationships.

8

The Fourth Step:
Learning to Love

Hail to loving concern for transmigrating beings
Who are powerless like a bucket traveling up and down a well
Through initially exaggerating oneself, "I,"
And then generating attachment for things, "This is mine."

—CHANDRAKIRTI

The fourth step, the generation of love, is described in this and the next three chapters. In this chapter we explore how beings suffer—first applying this understanding to ourselves and then extending it to others. The next chapter gives further detail about how troublesome emotions arise, drawing a clear distinction between love and attachment. In chapter 10, love freed of bias and attachment is shown to be the basis of human rights. Chapter 11 offers a set of exercises for expanding ordinary feelings of love and concern beyond their usual biased limits in ever-widening spheres.

BECOMING A FRIEND TO ALL

A loving altruistic attitude has only one face, kindness to others. However, this altruism helps others and yourself, both right now and in the long run. As the Tibetan lama Kunu Tenzin Gyelsten said, "If you want to be a friend of all people, generate love and compassion. If you want to be a spiritual guide for all people, generate love and compassion. If you want to help everyone, generate love and compassion." Even if you searched for eons to find the best method to achieve permanent happiness, you would find that the only way is to generate love and compassion.

By becoming truly aware of others and developing respect for them, we ourselves become much happier and more satisfied, which itself has the outward effect of creating an atmosphere of peace. For example, if in a room full of people someone becomes angry and begins shouting, the atmosphere becomes tense for everyone. However, if every person in a group feels and demonstrates warm feelings and respect for one another, the atmosphere is peaceful and harmonious. The external emanates from the internal. If your motivation is coarse and rude, it will be felt no matter how pleasurable the circumstances.

Your internal state is most paramount. If you become overwhelmed by mental discomfort, external things will not help at all. However, if internally there is love, warmth, and kindheartedness, external problems can be accepted and faced more easily.

It is doubtful that problems can be solved with anger. Although it may lead to temporary success with regard to the immediate aim and yield some satisfaction for a brief period, ultimately anger will cause further difficulties. (There is no need to enumerate the many instances of this in the last century and again in this century.) With anger all actions are swift. When we face problems with sincere concern for others, success may take longer, but it will be longer lasting.

It is particularly saddening nowadays to realize that many persons in dire distress are not being helped because of political considerations. Some suffer indirectly from the effects of governments putting too much money into armaments and, due to this, neglecting basic needs such as agriculture; the result is that when a natural disaster hits, the situation is hopeless. Others suffer directly from neglect out of discrimination against a community. If one American soldier is killed, it is immediately known, but few bother about how many civilians or combatants are killed on the other side. All of the killed are persons, each valuing his own life.

That people in need are ignored or abandoned for political reasons reveals what we are lacking—though we are intelligent and powerful, strong enough to exploit peoples and destroy the world, we lack real kindness and love. There is an Indian saying: "When an arrow has hit, there is no time to ask who shot it, or what kind of arrow it was." Similarly, when we encounter human suffering, it is important to respond with commiseration rather than to question the politics of those we help. Instead of asking whether their country is enemy or friend, we must think, These are human beings; they are suffering, and they have a right to happiness equal to our own.

STOPPING HARMING

This body will likely not last longer than one hundred or so years, even if we are fortunate. It is not something that can go on to a future lifetime. Its finitude means that physical qualities such as strength and agility have a limit. It is important to work on those limitless qualities that will be valuable beyond this lifetime. Attained through mental contemplation, these refined attitudes will also enrich this life.

Buddhist practices for training the mind can be summed up in two sentences: "If you are able, you should help others. If you are not able, you should at least not harm others." Both are based on love and compassion. First you must gain control over a tendency to harm, voluntarily restraining hurtful physical and verbal actions. The principal physical nonvirtues are killing, stealing, and sexual misconduct; the principal verbal nonvirtues are lying, divisive talk, harsh speech, and senseless chatter; the principal mental nonvirtues are covetousness, harmful intent, and wrong views. These ten cause suffering both for others and for you.

Killing means to end the life of a sentient being, either through your own actions or through compelling another to do it. Sometimes it stems from desire, as in killing an animal out of attachment to meat. Other times it is due to enmity, as in revenge, or it can even be due to rank confusion, as in thinking that animal sacrifice is beneficial. Every one of us has the potential to commit a crime like murder. As long as desire, hatred, attachment, jealousy, or ignorance are present, crime is possible.

Stealing arises mainly from desire—to take someone else's possession by deceit (as when a shopkeeper uses inaccurate scales), by force (mugging), or by burglary.

Sexual misconduct is motivated mainly by desire to copulate with an unsuitable partner, as in adultery or rape.

Lying arises from a motivation to dissemble, as in saying to another person, "I saw such and such," when you did not. You can mislead with words or with physical gestures.

Divisive speech intends to divide others who are in harmony or to cause further disagreement between enemies seeking reconciliation. It can be done overtly, covertly with deception, or indirectly through implication.

Harsh speech arises from wanting to say something unpleasant—usually out of hatred—about another person either directly to the person's face, covertly as in jest, or indirectly through gossip.

Senseless talk is usually driven by obscuration and obliviousness. To distract with idle chatter those who are trying to practice spiritual development is particularly destructive both to oneself and others.

Covetousness is repeatedly wishing for another's possessions. Arising mainly from desire, it is particularly harmful when you have no shame or embarrassment about it and do not try to stop it.

Harmful intent arises from hatred, as in the intention to kill another in battle; from jealousy, as in wanting to harm a rival; or from an unwillingness to forgive an enemy. Harmful intent has particularly powerful effects when it is considered a good quality that does not need to be corrected.

Wrong views are long-standing notions that virtues and ill deeds are not the causes of happiness and suffering respectively, and the denial that spiritual practice is effective. Wrong views come to fullness when you decide to look no further for the truth.

It is important to understand that counterproductive actions of body and speech do not just arise by themselves, but spring from dependence upon mental motivation. The influence of faulty states of mind causes faulty actions to be produced. Thus, to control negative physical and verbal actions, it is necessary to get at their root, the mind, and tame it. This level of the practice of love can be included within one sentence: "Do not harm others."

HELPING

The next level begins when you can bring these destructive factors somewhat under your control, giving you a better chance to help others. Altruism is the spirit out of which we choose to take action and give aid that brings happiness to others. Even a small experience of altruism brings a measure of mental peace right away. If altruism is the heart of good deeds, then great love and great compassion are the heart of such deeds. The truly altruistic person is moved by the suffering of each and every sentient being and wishes to join them with happiness and its causes and to free them from suffering and its causes.

Perhaps a selfish person is far superior to an animal, since animals are bound in such great misery, but both place their own welfare at the center of all thought and activity. Animals eat and drink to fulfill their own superficial purposes. People merely involved in their own progress lack the magnificence of those who are willing to dwell in the blazing fire of the pains of the world in order to remove even one type of suffering from a single sentient being. Such people are powerful, effective, wise, and possess unusually great strength of feeling.

Those training in great love *should* forsake self-centeredness and engage in the Buddha's practice, the root of which is compassion. You may be thinking, Love is indeed very profound, but I do not have the skill to practice it; I will focus my efforts on practices aimed at getting myself out of cyclic existence instead. On one hand, this is true, because you should choose a path of development appropriate to your ability. On the other hand, there is great advantage in attempting the highest degree of love you can. Even if you cannot actually implement the practices of love and compassion, merely hearing about them establishes powerful predispositions for future success. This can be amplified by planting prayer-wishes aspiring to altruism. Do not be discouraged; it is difficult to absorb such a profound perspective. Be courageous and think of your future potential. It is particularly important to do the best you can.

As the eighth-century Indian scholar-yogi Shantideva says in *A Guide to the Bodhisattva Way of Life,* there is immeasurable benefit even in wishing that all sentient beings be freed from a single suffering, such as a headache:

If even those who think, "I will clear away
Just the headaches of living beings,"
Have such a beneficial intention

That they gain immeasurable merit,
Then what is there to say
Of one who aspires to clear away
The immeasurable unhappiness of each being
And to endow each with immeasurable good
    qualities?

In a former lifetime while Buddha was an ordinary being before he became enlightened, he was reborn in a hell where, due to his former negative actions (karma), a device appeared on the top of his head and began churning up his brain. Immediately reflecting on the fact that this suffering was caused by his own earlier behavior, he contemplated other sentient beings who were suffering in a similar manner and made a wish that through his own pain all other beings could be relieved of all such pain. At that moment, the device lifted off his head; he was freed from that hell and reborn as a human.

If such great benefit arises from wishing that all beings be freed from a single type of suffering, think how amazingly beneficial it is to wish that all beings be freed from all suffering. As Nagarjuna says, there is merit in making donations to poor monastics, but love is even more powerful:

Even three times a day to offer
Three hundred pots of food to the needy
Does not match a portion of the merit
In one instant of love.

Even after many eons of rebirths, it is difficult to follow the auspicious words teaching this good path. Yet it is truly wonderful that we are able to admire and to practice such a path. The greatness of Tibetan culture lies in the detail of its teachings on how to cultivate love and compassion.

Some people think it is the nature of Tibetan people to be relaxed and to uphold good character, even though they are in a state of unusual suffering in an occupied nation. But the Tibetan approach arises from a way of thinking, a willingness to use bad circumstances on the spiritual path. Most Tibetans are not distressed; their inner freedom from anxiety shows itself outwardly as an easygoing manner.

Among practitioners, the best are those whose compassion extends even to a bug. It is perhaps in this respect that people notice something different about the Tibetan people. Indeed, some Tibetans kill animals while reciting a mantra like *om mani padme hum,* which is supposed to be repeated with the aim of cleansing various types of afflictive emotions in themselves and other sentient beings that lead to uncontrolled rebirth. But in general Tibetans are quite compassionate and merciful. For instance, most Tibetans look down on hunting, whereas in some Buddhist countries hunting is not considered bad. It is certainly not that Tibetans already have developed a high degree of altruism, but they do have a healthy sense of it. The teaching of compassion was widely disseminated in Tibet, and over time its people have internalized the intention to become enlightened in order to be more effective in helping others.

You should realize your great fortune at having encountered such an altruistic teaching and understand how important it is to put it into practice, if only as something you wish to develop. Even those who do not know much about spiritual development can appreciate that those who possess an other-directed attitude have great power of mind. In Buddhism, such beings are called bodhisattvas—those who are heroically intent (*sattva*) on achieving enlightenment (*bodhi*) in order to help others more effectively.

Ultimately bodhisattvas seek to establish each sentient being in Buddhahood. For the sake of others they are willing to give freely of their own resources, stores of virtuous karma that would yield pleasant results for themselves, and anything else that might be appropriate, without even the slightest feeling that "This is mine." They consider the welfare of others in all aspects of their own behavior, no matter what activity of body, speech, or mind they are engaging in. Even their inhalation and exhalation of breath serve others. These persons do indeed have unusual strength of mind to generate such altruism. This is why bodhisattvas are known as "*heroes* contemplating enlightenment."

Although it is difficult right away to achieve the full scope of altruism, you can work on beneficial predispositions toward it. Even if those who know little or nothing about spiritual development work at this attitude—which indeed is the sole path of the Buddhas, past, present, and future—they can eventually realize enlightenment, overcoming both the obstacles to liberation from the round of pain, and the barriers to full knowledge.

KNOWING HOW YOU AND OTHERS SUFFER

The cultivation of love requires understanding that all beings want happiness, and all beings are beset by suffering. Without identifying every kind of suffering, there is no way for love to be anything but partial. It is easy to feel a degree of love and compassion for a person in an obviously destitute situation, but it is difficult to commiserate with someone living in prosperity. This is a sign that we have not grasped the scope of suffering, that we have not understood what cyclic existence means.

What kinds of suffering do we undergo? Ordinary pain, suffering from change, and the unfortunate results of pervasive conditioning. We all know mental and physical pain—from headaches to back pain to sore feelings. Everyone wants to be free of it. The suffering from change is much harder to recognize. The simple fact that most ordinary pleasures easily turn into pain if overused shows that these temporary pleasures have an underlying nature of pain. For instance, if a good meal really had an inner nature of pleasure, then no matter how much we ate, we would feel happier and happier. However, when we eat too much of even the finest foods, we suffer. It is difficult to think of a pleasurable experience that, if overindulged in, does *not* have an inner nature of pain.

Beyond ordinary pain and the suffering of change, there is a much deeper level of suffering that is the hardest to recognize as such—that is, as something we need to overcome. Called "pervasive conditioning," it is the fact that our mind and body do not operate completely under our own control but under the influences of karma (tendencies created by previous actions) and emotions such as lust and hatred. In ordinary life we are born from and into the pervasive influence of karma and afflictive emotions. Even when we do not think we are feeling anything, we are under the influence of causes and conditions beyond our control—stuck in a cycle that is prone to suffering. When you realize how this cycle makes you susceptible to all sorts of unwanted events, you want to get rid of it as much as you would want to remove a speck of dust from your eye.

Suffering is a disease we all have. By diagnosing these three types of suffering, we can, over time, get a grasp on the full scope of the disease.

THE REVOLVING DOOR OF CONSCIOUSNESS

Since ordinary consciousness leads to suffering, let us take a look at different states of mind. The mind of ordinary activities is very coarse. When we fall asleep and dream, there is a subtler level of consciousness. In heavy, dreamless sleep there is another, more subtle type of consciousness. These three states of mind all occur while the body is still breathing, whereas in fainting there are occasions when breath stops, and the mind becomes even more subtle.

Finally, at death the subtlest of minds is manifest. When the force of karma that drives your present lifetime is spent, you will die. During this passage warmth gradually moves from the extremities of the body toward the heart, where an extremely subtle consciousness manifests itself before consciousness finally exits.

When this most subtle consciousness ceases, the intermediate state between lives begins. At this time, as an intermediate being between your former and future lives, you take on the form of your next lifetime and seek a place of rebirth. If you are to be reborn as a human, you arrive at the place where the man and woman having the karma of being your parents are lying together. You approach with lust, desiring the mother if you are to be reborn as a boy and desiring the father if you are to be reborn as a girl. You rush to them to engage in sex. When you cannot slake your desire, you become angry, and your life as an intermediate being ends. You are reborn to your next lifetime.

Once again, you are born, age, become sick, and die. The same process repeats over and over. Even between lives you accumulate karma every minute.

What causes this succession of many forms of suffering? Distressing emotions—mainly the three poisons of lust, hatred, and ignorance—and actions flowing from those afflictions, such as the ten nonvirtues discussed earlier.

Meditation

1. Reflect on the fact that in your own life you naturally want to overcome the obvious pains of sickness, aging, and death. Think of particular physical and mental pains.

2. Think about ordinary pleasures. Are they pleasurable in and of themselves? Or is it true that, indulged continuously, they turn into pain? If so, this reveals the deeper nature of pain.

3. Consider how nice it would be to be beyond being deceived by ordinary pleasures.

4. Recall a pleasure that turned into pain. Reflect on how the deeper nature of the pleasure revealed it-

self. Determine that in the future when a situation turns painful, you will realize that its inner nature has shown itself.

5. Consider that you are caught in a pervasive process of conditioning beyond your control, and see how it makes you susceptible to the karma and afflictive emotions that are forms of suffering. When you want to remove this conditioning as much as you want to get rid of physical pain like a particle in your eye and mental pain like the sorrow of separation from friends, you will understand the full scope of suffering in the cyclic life.

EXTENDING THIS UNDERSTANDING TO OTHERS

By understanding the range and depth of your own suffering, you gain a measure of progress toward turning away from overindulging in the pleasurable appearances of this lifetime and from striving too vigorously for fortunate situations in future lifetimes. Instead, you begin seeking liberation from the whole process of cyclic existence. The search for liberation should be infused with altruism. Otherwise, there is danger that the mind will be diverted toward wanting a state of solitary peace and freedom from suffering for yourself.

Extend the realization of the various forms of your cyclic existence to other beings and develop love and compassion for them. Dedicate yourself to relieving others from suffering and helping them attain happiness. As the fourteenth-century Tibetan scholar-yogi Tsongkhapa says,

> If your mind has not been affected by thinking about the ways that you yourself wander in cyclic existence, then when you think about these sufferings in other sentient beings, there is no way that you as a beginner can find their pain unbearable. Therefore, first you should think about these in yourself, and afterward meditate on them in other sentient beings.

Reflection on how others are trapped in cyclic existence the same way you are will increase your natural compassion. You and all sentient beings want happiness and do not want suffering. No matter how important you are, you are only one person. Therefore, your aim in seeking to attain full personal development, mental and physical, should be to assist vast numbers of sentient beings to gain relief and freedom. This is the motivation that a spiritual practitioner needs to bring to every endeavor.

Meditation

1. Bring to mind a friend and reflect on how this person suffers from mental and physical pain, suffers from mistakenly seeing temporary pleasures as having an inner nature of happiness, and suffers from being caught in a process of death and rebirth outside of her control, just as you are.

2. Extend this reflection to more and more friends, one by one.

3. Extend it further to several neutral persons, one by one.

4. Consider how the least of your enemies suffers from mental and physical pain, suffers from mistakenly seeing only temporary pleasures as having an inner nature of happiness, and suffers from being caught in a process of death and rebirth outside of his control, just as you are.

5. Slowly extend this to more and more of those who have harmed you or your friends.

You will find that over the course of weeks and months, your attitude toward others will become healthier and more realistic. Lust and hatred are unrealistic. Love and compassion are realistic. Artificial barriers will disappear.

9

The Difference Between
Love and Attachment

Like salt water, pleasurable things
Increase attachment no matter how much they are used.
The altruistic practice by viewing them
As like a summer rainbow, appearing to be
beautiful but untrue,
Thereby avoiding attachment and lust.

—BODHISATTVA TOKMAY SANGPO

To generate true love, you need to know how it differs from attachment. Ordinary love and compassion are intertwined with attachment, because their motivations are selfish: you care about certain people because they temporarily help you or your friends. As Nagarjuna's *Precious Garland* says:

Thought involved with attachment to others
Is an intention to help or not to help

Due to being affected by desire
Or an intent to harm.

Because such love and compassion are under the sway of attachment, they cannot be extended to enemies, only friends—your spouse, children, parents, and so forth. Whereas if love and compassion thrive within the clear recognition of the importance and rights of others, they will reach even those who would do you harm. From childhood I have had a tendency toward love and compassion, but it was biased. When two dogs were fighting, I would have strong feelings for the one who lost. Even when two bugs fought, I had strong concern for the smaller one, but would be angry at the winner. That shows that my love and compassion were biased.

In turning away from attachment, you need not ignore essential needs, such as food, shelter, and sleep. Rather, you should separate yourself from superficial distractions that elicit such exclamations as, "This is wonderful!" "I must have this!" "Oh, if I only could have this!" When you give your life over to such thoughts, finery and money become more attractive than spiritual development; distressing emotions increase, leading to trouble, disturbing yourself and those around you, while you figure out ways to satisfy these emotions, causing yet more trouble. Driven ragged by attachment, you find no comfort.

The best way to overcome counterproductive attachments is to realize that the very nature of life is that what has gathered will eventually disperse—parents, children, brothers, sisters, and friends. No matter how much friends love each other, eventually they must part. The mistake is to see these situations as inherently pleasurable. Attachment is built on this misperception and will always cause more pain.

Good fortune is not permanent; consequently, it is dangerous to become too attached to things going well. An outlook of permanence is ruinous. When the present becomes your preoccupation, the future does not matter, which undermines your motivation to engage in compassionate practices for the future enlightenment of others. An outlook of impermanence helps. By seeing that the true nature of things is disintegration, you will not be shocked by change when it occurs, not even death.

HOW TROUBLESOME
EMOTIONS ARISE

Lust and hatred are generated within a conception of ourselves as being very solid. Once there is a solidly existent, palpable, overly concrete "I," there is discrimination from the other—once there is "I," there also is "you." Discrimination is followed by attachment to your solid self and anger toward the other side. As the seventh-century Indian scholar-yogi Chandrakirti says,

> Beings are powerless like a bucket traveling up and
>   down a well
> Through initially exaggerating oneself, "I,"
> And then generating attachment for things, "This is
>   mine."

Beings who first conceive of a solidly existent "I" also conceive of solidly existent things that can be owned. Through the force of this process—discrimination of self and other and attachment to objects—we wander through better and worse states of cyclic existence, like a bucket traveling powerlessly up and down a well.

It is crucial to identify in your own experience that

persons and things appear as if they exist in and of themselves, but they do not. If the person or object appears pleasant, two powerful streams of attraction are produced—attachment to yourself and attachment to the pleasurable person or object. Your attachment to the feeling of pleasure itself draws you into distressing actions and thereby into cyclic problems. As long as you deny the true nature of people and things, you will believe that both inherently exist. It will not be long before desire and hatred enter the picture.

THE NATURE OF ATTACHMENT

Attachment increases desire, without producing any satisfaction. There are two types of desire, unreasonable and reasonable. The first is an affliction founded on ignorance, but the second is not. To live, you need resources; therefore, desire for sufficient material things is appropriate. Such feelings as, "This is good; I want this. This is useful," are not afflictions. It is also desirable to achieve altruism, wisdom, and liberation. This kind of desire is suitable; indeed, all human development comes out of desire, and these aspirations do not have to be an affliction.

For instance, when you have developed an affinity for all sentient beings, and desire that they all should have happiness, such desire is valid because it is unbiased. It covers *all* sentient beings. It is likely that our present love, being limited to friends and family, is heavily influenced by ignorant attachment. It is biased.

Counterproductive desire is unreasonable attachment to things. This inevitably leads to lack of contentment. Ask yourself if you really need most of these things, and the answer is no. This type of desire has no limit, no way to satisfy itself. It leads ultimately to suffering. You must put a brake on this kind of desire.

In the early stages of practice, it is difficult to distinguish between useful desire and afflictive desire. A practitioner might feel love and compassion but still hold the ignorant idea that he himself and the object of that love and compassion are inherently established. At the beginning of spiritual practice even ignorance can serve as an aid to enlightenment. When you first cultivate love and compassion, even if ignorance and attachment are involved, it would be a mistake to stop practicing; the only good choice is to continue. To overcome attachment you cannot just withdraw your mind from objects. Instead, you must overcome attachment through the practice of realizing the opposite of ignorance.

However, when you have attachment to *material* things, it is best to desist from those very activities that promote more attachment. Satisfaction is helpful when it comes to material things, but not with respect to spiritual practice. Objects to which we become attached are something to be discarded, whereas spiritual progress is something to be adopted—it can be developed limitlessly, even in old age.

Although in the beginning it is difficult to distinguish between afflictive and nonafflictive desire, through sustained investigation and analysis you can gradually identify ignorance and the afflictive emotions, making your practice more and more pure. Attachment is one-sided, narrowly focused on yourself for just the short term; the more attached you become, the more biased and narrow you become. Even small things will disturb you. Detachment involves the absence of that kind of narrow-mindedness, but it does not mean that you have given up interest. Because we need a wide range of things, we need detachment; so in order to be more open-minded, more holistic, detachment is needed. Attachment shuts things out. It is an obstacle. Students who become overly attached to one subject become lopsided; many subjects need to be studied.

The general procedure of narrow-minded worldly life is summed up by what are called "the eight worldly concerns":

like/dislike
gain/loss
praise/blame
fame/disgrace

The worldly way of life is to be unhappy when the four unfavorable ones—dislike, loss, blame, and disgrace—happen to you or your friends, but to be pleased when these happen to your enemies. These results are all based on how people act, whereas true love and compassion are based not on actions but on the crucial fact that these sentient beings want happiness and do not want suffering, like you, and thus are all equal. Some actions are positive, and some are negative, but the agents of those actions are all sentient beings with aspirations to happiness. We always need to look from that angle. Actions are secondary, since they are sometimes positive and sometimes negative—always changing—whereas there is never any change in the fact that beings want happiness and do not want suffering.

When a shocking event happens, whether during the day or when dreaming, our immediate response is "I," not Tibetan, not American, or any other nationality; not Buddhist, not Hindu, or any other system, but just "I." This shows us the basic human level. On that important level all are the same. Little children do not bother about religion and nationality, rich or poor; they just want to play together. At a young age the sense of oneness of humanity is much more fresh. As we grow older, we make a lot of distinctions; a lot of artificial creations that are actually secondary become more important, and basic human concern diminishes. That is a problem.

Love thrown into bias by lust and hatred eventually must be stopped. Love influenced by afflictive desire necessarily brings with it hatred at what opposes it, and along with that comes jealousy and all sorts of problems. Though lust itself does not directly harm, it indirectly brings about all the forces that harm. This is why the process of expanding love begins with developing equanimity, after which the main point is not whether a particular person is good or bad to you but the fact that the person is the same as yourself in wanting happiness and not wanting suffering. Since this desire resides in all sentient beings, your awareness of it can apply to everyone, making the basis of your love very stable. Once you put the emphasis on their similarity to yourself, love has a solid foundation that does not vacillate depending on temporary circumstances.

In my own practice, when I consider, for instance, a particular person who is currently torturing Tibetans in my homeland, I do not concentrate on that person's bad attitude and bad behavior but reflect on the fact that this is a human who, like myself, wants happiness and does not want suffering, but is voluntarily bringing pain to himself and intentionally destroying his own happiness. When I look at things from this perspective, my response is love and compassion. I choose that perspective, that angle. If I considered the person as an enemy harming Tibetans, love would not be my response.

One of the chief reasons why lust and hatred arise is that we are too attached to this lifetime. We want to believe it is permanent, that it will last forever, and so we concentrate too much on temporary circumstances and place too much value on material goods. The only way to get around this is to reflect on the fact that all things pass—you too will pass away. As the thirteenth- and fourteenth-century Tibetan adept Tokmay Sangpo says,

> It is a practice of the altruistic to diminish the hold
>   of this life—
> Close friends, who companied together for a long
>   time, separate,
> The wealth and articles achieved with striving are
>   left behind,
> And the guesthouse of the body is left by the guest
>   of consciousness.

No matter how long we live, at most around a hundred years, eventually we must die, losing this valuable human life. And it could happen at any time. This life will disintegrate, no matter how much prosperity we have. No amount of wealth can buy an extension of your life. On the day of death nothing you have accumulated can help; you have to leave it all behind. In this respect, the death of a rich person and the death of a wild animal are alike.

Under the sway of attachment the object appears to be good through and through, but in reality it is not that way. When attachment starts to develop, try to find negative qualities in the object of your desire. Once attachment has set in, it is very difficult to suppress; your best chance is to try distracting your attention from the object, perhaps even physically leaving it behind.

Attachment to a close friend can be so strong that it leads to upsetting that loved one at the time of her dying. Grasping at a person's hand, tearfully embracing her, even moaning in front of her—these actions can ruin any chance of the dying person's generating a virtuous frame of mind by causing her to cling to this lifetime. A friend should provide conditions for virtuous thoughts by reminding the dying person of religious instructions and practices with gentle speech. The dying person should be reminded that there will be many unusual appearances caused by karma during death. It is crucial to understand that there is no point in being attached to the pleasant appearances or angered by the unpleasant ones.

A STRONG WILL

It is important to aspire to bring about the well-being of others and to develop that aspiration so that it becomes stronger and stronger. This is not attachment, because it is not mixed with afflictive emotions. The strong aspiration arises from detachment.

A strong ego is needed, but without becoming egotistical. You need a strong will to achieve the good. To make a wish that you become able to help all beings throughout space, you need a strong self; with a weak self such an intention is impossible. This kind of desire is reasonable and is not attachment. It is to be adopted in practice. Unreasonable desire is to be diminished and discarded because of its narrowness.

MAKING THIS LIFE MEANINGFUL

Loosening your hold on this lifetime does not mean that you should stop taking care of yourself and others. When I suggest that you view the body as having a nature of suffering, it does not mean that you should neglect the body. Your body can help you achieve great aims. As Shantideva's *Guide to the Bodhisattva Way of Life* says,

> Relying upon the boat of a human body,
> Free yourself from the great river of suffering.

The marvelous prosperity and boundless resources of any life in cyclic existence will ultimately deteriorate, but the body should be viewed as fortuitous for bringing about others' welfare. As such it has to be nourished and developed within an attitude of nonattachment. It is necessary to take care of our present condition within a state of mind turned toward future lifetimes.

Buddha teaches that one should not practice extremes. Torturing yourself is an extreme that should be avoided. As Nagarjuna's *Precious Garland of Advice* says,

Practice is not done
By mortifying the body,
Since you have not forsaken injuring others
And are not helping others.

When you disregard the basic needs of the body, you harm the many sentient organisms that live within the body. You should also avoid the opposite extreme of living in great luxury. It is possible to make use of good food, clothing, residence, and furnishings without producing afflictive emotions such as attachment, pride, and arrogance. The crucial point is the control of internal factors such as lust and attachment; external factors are not in and of themselves good or bad. It is not suitable if attachment increases toward even mediocre food, clothing, and so forth.

Contentment is the key. If you have contentment with material things, you are truly rich. Without it, even if you are a billionaire, you will not have happiness. You will always feel hungry and want more and more and more, making you not rich but poor. If you seek contentment externally, it will never happen. Your desire will never be fulfilled. Our texts speak of a king who gained control over the world, at which point he began thinking about taking over the lands of the gods. In the end his good qualities were destroyed by pride.

Contentment is necessary for happiness, so try to be satisfied with adequate food, clothing, and shelter. For a layperson sexual excitement is generally not considered to be wrong, but too much emphasis on it can bring disaster. Everything needs to be felt and enacted in a balanced way. This is essential. Too much excitation and sexual attachment can be the seed of divorce.

Tolerance is also necessary. When Buddha was meditating before he became enlightened, seemingly external evil forces came to torment him. He did not respond with aggression or threaten military action. He just meditatively cultivated love and compassion, and through that practice destroyed the force of evil.

Giving up attachment to the world does not mean

that you separate yourself from it. When you generate a reasoned desire for the happiness of others, your human-ness increases in strength. As you become more detached from the world, rather than denying your humanity, you become more humane. Buddha himself set forth vows of altruism for laypersons and for monastics, which means that he envisioned practitioners with families. The very purpose of Buddhist practice is to help others. In order to do so, you must remain in society.

IO

Love as the Basis of Human Rights

Knowing the concordance
Of actions and their effects,
Always help beings in fact.
Just that will help yourself.

—NAGARJUNA, *PRECIOUS GARLAND OF ADVICE*

It is human to have a valid feeling of "I," and it follows naturally from that feeling that we want to pursue happiness and avoid suffering. This is our birthright, and it does not need further justification. All other sentient beings also wish to be free of suffering, so if you have the right to overcome suffering, then other sentient beings naturally have the same human right. Then what is the difference between self and other? There is a great difference in number, if not in kind. Others are more numerous than you. You are just one, and the number of other sentient beings is countless.

Who is more important, you or others? I am just one Buddhist monk, but other people are infinite in number. The conclusion is clear; even if minor suffering happens to all others, its range is infinite, whereas when something happens to me, it is limited to just one person. When we look at others in this way, oneself is not so important.

Out of ten sick people, who does not want happiness? No one. They all want to be freed from their illness. In the practice of altruism, there is no possible reason for an exception, treating one person better while neglecting others. In this world alone there are several billion, who, like yourself, do not want suffering and do want happiness.

From your own viewpoint, remember that all sentient beings have helped you over the course of past lifetimes and will help you again in future ones. Thus, there is no reason to treat some better and others worse.

We all have a nature of suffering and impermanence. Once we recognize our community in deprivation, there is no sense in being belligerent with each other. Consider a group of prisoners who are about to be executed. During their stay together in prison, all of them will meet their end. There is no sense in quarreling out their remaining days. All of us are bound by the same nature of suffering and impermanence. Under such circumstances, there is absolutely no reason to fight with each other.

Meditation

1. Notice your natural experience of "I," as in "I want this," "I do not want that."

2. Recognize that it is natural to want happiness and not to want pain. This is correct and does not require further justification, validated simply by the fact that you innately want happiness and do not want suffering.

3. Based on this natural aspiration, you have the right to obtain happiness and to get rid of suffering.

4. Further, just as you have this feeling and this right, others equally have the same feeling, and the same right.

5. Reflect on the fact that the difference between yourself and others is that you are just one single person, whereas others are limitless.

6. Pose this question: Should everyone be used for my attainment of happiness, or should I help others gain happiness?

7. Imagine yourself, calm and reasonable, looking to the right at another version of yourself—but this self is overly proud, never thinking of others' welfare, concerned only with its own self, willing to do most anything to satisfy it.

8. Visualize to your left a number of destitute people unrelated to you, needy and in pain.

9. Now you in the middle are an unbiased sensible person. Consider how both sides want happiness and want to get rid of pain; in this way, they are equal, the same. And both have the right to accomplish these goals.

10. But think:

> The selfishly motivated person on the right is just one person, whereas the others are far greater in number, even limitless. Who is more important? This single self-centered, stupid person, or the group of poor, helpless people?

Which side will you join? As the unbiased person in the middle, you will naturally favor the greater number of suffering people; there is no way to avoid the overwhelming needs of the multitude, especially in contrast to that one proud, stupid character.

11. Reflect: If I, as just one person, take advantage of the majority, it is truly contrary to my humanity. Indeed, to sacrifice one hundred dollars for the sake of one dollar is very foolish, but to spend one dollar for the sake of one hundred dollars is very wise.

12. Thinking this way, decide:

> I am going to direct my energies to the many rather than to this one selfish person. Every part of the body is equally considered to be body and to be protected from pain; so all sentient beings are to be equally protected from suffering.

For me this meditation is particularly effective. It is very clear that all of the troubles on this earth are ultimately due to egotism and self-cherishing. You can understand the principles of this meditation from your own experience right in this lifetime—that self-cherishing leads to ill deeds, even murder, and that other-cherishing leads to virtues such as abandoning killing, stealing, sexual misconduct, lying, divisive talk, harsh speech, and gossip.

With this meditation, even if you are not aware of the kindness of others, you can learn to cherish others. Remember that you cherish yourself naturally, not out of any sense that you have been kind to yourself. From the very fact that you cherish your life, you want to get rid of suffering and gain happiness. In the same way, all sentient beings naturally cherish themselves, and from this they want to get rid of suffering and gain happiness. We are all the same; the difference is that others are many, whereas you are just one person. Even if you could use all other beings for your own aims, you would not be happy. But if you, just one being, serve others as fully as you can, this work will be a source of inner joy.

It is easy to understand that you will lose out if you neglect everyone else due to overemphasizing yourself and that you will gain greatly from valuing others as you cherish yourself. Since these facts are confirmed by our own experience, I find this meditation to have great impact.

Take these reflections to heart, and you will gradually

become less selfish and have more respect for others. With such an attitude, real love and compassion can grow.

ENCAPSULATION

Many types of valid consciousnesses derive from basic, natural, and obvious perception. All of us have an innate "I," although if we try to locate this "I," we get into a lot of difficulties. This sense of "I" gives us a well-founded aspiration to happiness and a wish not to suffer.

There are different levels of happiness and different kinds of suffering. Material things usually correspond to physical happiness, whereas spiritual development corresponds to mental happiness. Since our "I" has these two aspects—physical and mental—we need an inseparable combination of material progress and internal, or spiritual, progress. Balancing these is crucial to utilizing material progress and inner development for the good of human society.

Big schemes for world development arise from this wish to gain happiness and relieve suffering. But there are higher levels of happiness beyond these worldly forms, in which one seeks something longer-term, not just confined to this lifetime. Just as we need a long-range perspective that protects the environment, we need an internal long-range perspective that extends to future lifetimes.

I usually advise that even if you must be selfish, then be wisely selfish. Wise people serve others sincerely, putting the needs of others above their own. The ultimate result will be that you will get more happiness. The kind of selfishness that leads to fighting, killing, stealing, and using harsh words—forgetting other people's welfare, always thinking of yourself, "I, I, I"—will result in your own loss. Others may speak nice words in front of you, but behind your back they will not speak so nicely.

The practice of altruism is the authentic way of conducting human life, and is not limited to the religious. The crux of our existence is that, as human beings, we live purposeful, meaningful lives. Our purpose is to develop a warm heart. We find meaning in being a friend to everyone. The sole source of peace in the family, the country, and the world is altruism—love and compassion.

II

Widening the Circle of Love

_____

With love you will attain eight good qualities—
Gods and humans will be friendly,
Even non-humans will protect you,
You will have many mental and physical pleasures,
Poison and weapons will not harm you,
Without striving you will attain your aims,
And be reborn in a wonderful state.

—NAGARJUNA, *PRECIOUS GARLAND OF ADVICE*

Cultivating love advances the wish that sentient beings bereft of happiness meet with happiness and its causes. The aim now is to extend your sphere of love beyond its present scope. Such expansion will come naturally in your practice after having developed a sense of affinity with others who want happiness and do not want suffering. The previous steps have prepared you to easily extend warm feelings to more and more sentient beings, bringing them into your affections regardless of whether they are at present friends, neutral persons, or enemies.

Still, at the initial stages of practice you will have different levels of love—stronger for those who are, for the time being, closer to you and weaker for those who are, for the time being, not so close. As you practice and gradually progress, the force of your love will not discriminate between friend and enemy. Such all-pervasive, equal love cannot come right away; it must be cultivated. As I was saying earlier, in the initial stages of practice, love, compassion, faith, and so forth are often mixed with a little of the afflictive emotions. Techniques of contemplative reflection are needed to broaden the range of your love to envelop more and more beings.

CULTIVATING LOVE

It is easier to begin with friends, so let's start here to experience the change of heartfelt perspective as you consider them one by one.

1. Starting with your best friend, think:
    This person wants happiness but is bereft. How nice it would be if he could be imbued with happiness and all of its causes.

Meditate on this for a long period until you generate a sense of cherishing your best friend the way a mother cherishes her sweet child. Though this will be easy to do with such a good friend, take your time, and notice your feelings; they will be a model to extend to others.

2. Continue the same meditation with respect to more and more friends until this wish for happiness and for its causes is equally strong for all of them. One by one:

> This person wants happiness but is bereft. How nice it would be if she could be imbued with happiness and all of its causes.

If your feelings here are not as strong as they were for your best friend, revivify the impact of the earlier steps; reflect on the similarity of all your friends in wanting happiness and not wanting suffering; reflect that in the course of cyclic existence, they have all been your best friend—have been equally kind to you, and equally deserve reciprocation of that kindness.

3. Imagining a neutral being in front of you, deeply think:

> This person wants happiness but is bereft. How nice it would be if he could be imbued with happiness and all of its causes.

Make sure not to let the meditation flatten into merely words; the point of the words is transformation.

4. Continue the same meditation with respect to more and more neutral persons until this wish for happiness and for all its causes is equally strong for friends and neutral persons.

5. Imagining the least of your enemies in front of you, contemplate:

> This person wants happiness but is bereft. How nice it would be if she could be imbued with happiness and all of its causes.

Keep with this practice until you actually feel the same heartfelt wish for happiness and its causes for this person who has harmed you or your friends—until that wish is as strong as it is for friends and neutral persons.

6. Continue the same practice with respect to another enemy, such as someone who has bothered you at work or in public. With each new success, take on more and more enemies, gradually widening the scope of your love.

Such unbiased love is undeniably difficult, but if you practice this way with great determination, then day by day, week by week, month by month, your attitude will be transformed.

INTENSIFYING LOVE

Enhance the experience of intimately seeking others' well-being by adding a stronger wish, one that calls for their betterment to take effect. Use the same pattern as above.

1. Starting with your best friend, think:
   This person wants happiness but is bereft. May she be imbued with happiness and all its causes.

2. Extend the same wish to more and more friends until the call for happiness and for its causes is equally strong for all of them.

>   This person wants happiness but is bereft. May
>   he be imbued with happiness and all its causes.

3. Imagining a neutral being in front of you, think
    from the depths:

    >   This person wants happiness but is bereft. May
    >   she be imbued with happiness and all its causes.

4. Continue the same meditation with respect to
    more and more neutral persons until the call for
    happiness and for its causes is equally strong for
    friends and neutral persons.

5. Imagining the least of your enemies in front of
    you, contemplate:

    >   This person wants happiness but is bereft.
    >   May he be imbued with happiness and all its
    >   causes.

    Apply various reflections based on the earlier
    steps until you experience the same heartfelt long-
    ing for happiness and all its causes for this person
    who has harmed you or your friends—until it is as
    strong as it is for friends and neutral persons. This
    takes time.

6. Continue the same practice with respect to another enemy, someone who has irritated and upset you.

> This person wants happiness but is bereft. May she be imbued with happiness and all its causes.

When your feeling is strong and sincere, then consider another enemy, and then another, gradually widening the circle of your love. The effect is profound.

ASSUMING THE TASK

This generation of love and compassion for others changes you, but the beings who are the objects of these feelings are still suffering. Having generated two levels of love, your next step is to develop the stronger intention, "I will do whatever I can to cause her to be imbued with happiness and all the causes of happiness!" Here, you inhabit the strong determination not just to change your own attitude in mind but actually to help those beings become established in happiness through your own effort.

This high intention will endow you with great courage to take on the great task of the welfare of all sentient beings. When you have strength of mind, the greater the hardships are, the greater will be your determination and courage. Hardship will serve to sharpen your determination.

Where there is a will, there is a way, is indeed true. When we get entangled in a difficult situation, if our will, or courage, lessens, if we fall into laziness or feel inferior to the task, thinking that we could not possibly undo this difficulty, this diminishment of will cannot protect us from suffering and will likely make more. We must generate courage equal to the size of the difficulties we face.

The following technique deepens your will and sense of involvement:

1. Starting with your best friend, think:

    I will do whatever I can to cause her to be imbued with happiness and all the causes of happiness!

    Notice the strength of your feeling of involvement, the feeling that this matters to you.

2. Extend the same intention to more and more friends until your involvement in their attainment of happiness and all its causes is equally strong for all of them.

I will do whatever I can to cause him to be imbued with happiness and all the causes of happiness!

3. Imagining a neutral being in front of you, think from the depths:

   I will do whatever I can to cause her to be imbued with happiness and all the causes of happiness!

4. Continue the same meditation with respect to more and more neutral persons until your involvement in their attainment of happiness and all its causes is equally strong for friends and neutral persons.

5. Imagining the least of your enemies in front of you, contemplate:

   I will do whatever I can to cause him to be imbued with happiness and all the causes of happiness!

   Keep meditating until you experience—as strongly as you do for friends and neutral persons—the same deep involvement in his attainment of happiness and all its causes. This takes time.

6. Continue the practice with another enemy, some-one who has irritated and upset you:

> I will do whatever I can to cause her to be imbued with happiness and all the causes of happiness!

When your feeling is strong and sincere, then consider another enemy, then another, gradually widening the circle of your committed love. You will be amazed at the effects.

BOOSTER TECHNIQUE

In daily practice, reflect on the benefits of love, compassion, kindness, and so forth, then reflect on the disadvantages of anger. Such continuous thoughtful contemplation, the growing appreciation of love, revivifying and increasing—all have the effect of lessening our affinity for hatred and gaining our respect for love. Through the force of this understanding, even anger will change its aspect and be diminished.

• • •

This is the way to practice; with time, mental attitudes can change. All good qualities have to be sown and cultivated over months and years. You cannot expect to go to sleep tonight as an ordinary person and rise tomorrow with high realization.

12

The Fifth Step:
The Power of Compassion

Compassion is a mind having the single savor
Of mercy for all sentient beings.
From compassion all aims are achieved.

—NAGARJUNA, *PRECIOUS GARLAND OF ADVICE*

Along with love, compassion is the face of altruism. It is a feeling from deep in the heart that you cannot bear others' suffering without acting to relieve it. As compassion grows stronger, so does the willingness to commit yourself to the welfare of all beings, even if you have to do it alone. This is unbiased service toward all beings, no matter what their dispositions are. In the clarity of this commitment, you see that by achieving enlightenment yourself, you will finally be able to fulfill the hopes of everyone in your expanded circle of love. "I will do whatever I can to attain enlightenment for their sake," you decide. Compassion is the stone foundation of the altruistic intention to attain highest enlightenment in order to help all beings.

Great compassion is the root of altruistic action, the object of amazement to the world; there is no greater source of help and happiness. As long as you have compassion, you will be free of the deepest anxiety. The capacity to devote yourself to the welfare of others yields otherwise unobtainable power and potential for good. Generate great compassion, and you become a friend to all sentient beings, a companion to all other altruistic beings, and a cherished child of the enlightened.

COMPASSION AS SEED, WATER, AND HARVEST

Compassion itself is seen to be
The seed of a rich harvest, water for growth,
And the ripened state of long enjoyment.
Therefore, at the start I praise compassion.

— CHANDRAKIRTI

Compassion is crucial in the beginning, middle, and consummation of spiritual practice. It is like the seed of enlightenment. You need water, earth, and nutrients to grow crops—whether rice, barley, corn, or wheat. A rice seed can serve only as a cause of a rice shoot and cannot grow barley, so it is the uncommon cause of rice. Similarly, a compassionate motivation is the uncommon cause of the highest enlightenment, and thus it becomes the foundation of spiritual practice, like a seed. It is the beginning.

In the middle stages, when putting altruistic intention into practice, you discover that it is not easy to help even one sentient being overcome the manifest form of even one type of problem, not to mention overcoming its latent predispositions in the mind. Such improvement requires continuous effort. You might become tired and discouraged, but if you continue to develop compassion, you will not lose the altruistic dedication that you generated earlier. If you keep your compassion strong when you encounter difficult circumstances, your commitment will increase naturally. This is the importance of compassion in the middle stages: it is like water nurturing spiritual qualities that will in turn nurture others toward enlightenment.

Full enlightenment means that you are in the continual presence of great compassion; therefore you will not remain in solitary peace but will always be fully engaged in the welfare of others. Like the ripened state of a harvest to be enjoyed by multitudes, this is the importance of great compassion in the end.

Concern for others is a willingness to bear the burden of helping them achieve their own happiness. Such a courageous, unparalleled, altruistic assumption of this burden leads, over time, to aspiring to the levels of spiritual development in order to serve more effectively.

In Lhasa, Tibet, when giving teachings on love and compassion in my youth, I would be moved from deep inside. After first arriving as a refugee to Dharmsala, India, I was conducting an initiation ceremony, and I wept when reciting the stanza by Chandrakirti (given on page 134). Though I was deeply moved by contemplating the marvelous qualities of altruism, they felt like something distant, difficult for me to achieve. Around 1969, after gaining insight into how we exaggerate ourselves into being like a master and exaggerate things into being objects under our control, I saw that liberation is indeed possible because the ignorance that makes such exaggerations is simply wrong, and there is a counterforce—valid knowledge, wisdom—that can eliminate it.

Knowing that enlightenment was attainable, and after practicing Shantideva's *Guide to the Bodhisattva Way of*

Life in my late thirties, I gained enough experience that my sense that true love and compassion were at a distance changed, and I developed confidence that I could actually develop such altruism. Since then I have made some progress toward that goal.

Let me tell you a funny story about those tears. A person who was attending the ceremony and had not understood in the least why I cried went to see my junior tutor, Trijang Rinpoche, the next day. He reported that the Dalai Lama was extremely distressed during the ceremony, to the point where he cried. Trijang Rinpoche asked him, "Why was he crying?" He said, "He was depressed because he had had only one chance in Tibet to give this initiation." Trijang was amazed at the man's error. "Not only are you wrong that His Holiness gave this initiation only once in Tibet, but he would never be distressed over such a thing." I laughed and laughed when I heard the story.

HOW TO WIDEN THE CIRCLE OF CONCERN

Toward whom are you cultivating compassion? The answer is, Every sentient being, because everyone is afflicted with some form of suffering. In earlier meditations you developed an intimacy with other beings. First you recognized that you and they equally want happiness and do not want suffering; next you learned that over the continuum of lifetimes everyone has been your best friend, giving help to you joyfully; finally you saw that it is the very nature of society that others provide necessary services that help you, whether intentionally or not. If you did not have this empathetic perspective, then when you tried to understand the suffering of another through your own suffering, you might even take pleasure in an enemy's pain.

Several centuries ago, a monk happily heard that another monk whom he did not like had married, in violation of his monastic vows. The happy monk made some tea, invited his friends, and told them, "I have something good to tell you. Folks are saying that that monk has a woman." When the gossiper's lama learned what happened, he said, "This gossiper has accumulated more bad karma by liking it that another monk lost his vows than that monk himself did." As Tsongkhapa says,

In the world when suffering is seen in an enemy, not only is it not unbearable, but you delight in it. When a person who has neither helped nor harmed yourself is seen to suffer, you will in most cases pay no attention to that person. These reactions are due to not having a sense of affinity with respect to these persons.

However, when you see a friend suffer, it is unbearable, and the degree of unbearability is just as great as your affinity with that person. Therefore, it is an important essential to generate a sense of strong cherishing and affection for sentient beings.

No matter whether they are rich or poor, healthy or sick, young or old, it is crucial to have an abiding sense of others' dearness and their constant suffering.

It is easier to generate compassion while visualizing a sentient being who is very destitute, but we need also to reflect on persons who do not seem to be suffering at all, but who are in truth acting in ways that will eventually bring about manifest suffering. Extend this visualization and compassion to persons who have done such deeds in the past, accumulating negative karmic predispositions. Though the effects of their karma are not currently being experienced, these prosperous persons hold the causes of future pain as surely as if a cancerous tumor rested painlessly in their bodies. Expand the meditation again by reflecting on sentient beings who mistake the inner nature of what is only superficially pleasurable and must undergo the suffering of change. Finally, reflect on how all sentient beings are under the sway of pervasive suffering—bound in a process of conditioning beyond their control.

Steps of Meditation

Since it is easier to generate compassion toward friends, begin with a close friend.

1. Bring to mind a friend who has obvious pain, and think:

> Like me, this person wants happiness and does not want suffering, yet is stricken with such pain. If this person could only be free from suffering and the causes of suffering!

Analyze the ways this person suffers until you have a strong feeling of how wonderful it would be if she could be free from pain of all sorts, and stay with that feeling without analysis. When the feeling diminishes, think more on how the person suffers, and when this generates strong commiseration and a wish for her relief, stick to it without analysis. This is called alternating analytic meditation and stabilizing meditation. Perform the two back and forth, alternating so that the intensity of feeling remains strong. Eventually, the two types of meditation will assist and further each other without your having to switch between them.

2. Visualize in front of you a friend who, even though not stricken with immediate suffering, will suffer in the future due to heavy, counterproductive actions of the kind that we have all committed over the course of beginningless time. Think:

> Like me, this person wants happiness and does not want suffering, yet is stricken with such pain. If this person could only be free from suffering and the causes of suffering!

Alternate analytic and stabilizing meditation.

3. Slowly extend this meditation person by person, first with more friends, then with neutral persons, and finally with enemies, eventually including all sentient beings throughout space.

Extend the range of the meditation so that you are not limited to wishing that only a few beings be rid of suffering, or that all beings be freed from certain types of suffering. Wishing for the welfare of others is not partial and is not biased—it is a heartfelt wish that each and every sentient being be liberated from all sufferings and its causes.

By cultivating compassion first for friends, then neutral persons, and finally enemies, you can eventually grasp what it is to feel strong compassion for sentient beings in general. However, if initially you meditate on sentient beings in general without earnestly attending to individuals, you might get the impression of having compassion for all beings, but when an unfavorable circumstance such as being thwarted in something you want arises, you will demonstrate quite the opposite.

BOOSTER MEDITATION

It is also useful to imagine a helpless animal—a being of very limited ability with no protector—in a destitute state. Imagine such a creature in front of you and consider what it would be like to change places. Think:

> If I were in the position of this poor animal, could I bear it or not?

Try to feel what another being is feeling. This type of imaginative meditation is very helpful for fueling compassion.

INTENSIFYING COMPASSION

When you have made some progress, intensify the force of compassion by moving from "*If* this person could only be free from suffering and the causes of suffering!" to "*May* this person be free from suffering and the causes of suffering!"

1. Bring to mind a friend who is in obvious pain, and think:

    > Like me, this person wants happiness and does not want suffering, yet is stricken with such pain. May this person be free from suffering and the causes of suffering!

    Alternate analytic and stabilizing meditation.

2. Visualize in front of you a friend who, even though not stricken with obvious suffering, will suffer in the future due to heavy, counterproductive actions of the kind that we have all committed over the course of beginningless time. Think:

> Like me, this person wants happiness and does not want suffering, yet is stricken with such pain. May this person be free from suffering and the causes of suffering!

Alternate analytic and stabilizing meditation.

3. Slowly extend this meditation person by person, first to more friends, then to neutral persons, and finally to enemies, eventually including all sentient beings throughout space.

When you feel the full impact of this heightened wish, move on to the strongest level of compassion, which is the determination: "*I will help* this person be free from suffering and the causes of suffering!"

1. Bring to mind a friend who is in obvious pain, and think:

> Like me, this person wants happiness and does not want suffering, yet is stricken with such pain. I will help this person be free from suffering and the causes of suffering!

Alternate analytic and stabilizing meditation.

2. Visualize in front of you a friend who, even though not stricken with obvious suffering, will suffer in the future due to heavy, counterproductive actions of the kind that we have all committed over the course of beginningless time. Think:

   Like me, this person wants happiness and does not want suffering, yet is stricken with such pain. I will help this person be free from suffering and the causes of suffering!

   Alternate analytic and stabilizing meditation.

3. Slowly extend this meditation person by person, first to more friends, then to neutral persons, and finally to enemies, eventually including all sentient beings throughout space.

Through this process, true compassion will evolve. This is not common compassion mixed with attachment, wherein when some little thing goes wrong, we immediately get angry. True compassion is an awareness that all sentient beings should be freed from suffering.

HOW TO HANDLE ANGER

When others are mean and nasty to you, it is difficult to stay compassionate. Anger needs to be controlled, but not hidden from yourself. Recognize your reactions; do not deny them. If you do, your compassion will be superficial.

There are two classes of emotions. One class needs to be expressed, talked about. Take depression, for example. Perhaps someone close to you has died, and you are grieving privately. If instead of hiding your feelings, you express them openly, the overwhelming power of that sadness will be weakened. The other class of emotions includes anger, strong attachment, and strong desire; there is no natural end to these. For instance, if anger is expressed, tomorrow there may be more; whereas if you try to minimize your anger, it will weaken. We can see this in our own experience. Giving your anger the instrument of words and actions is like giving a child a pile of straw and a box of matches. Once lit, anger feeds off the air of exposure and can rage out of control. The only alternative is to control anger, and the way to do this is to think, What is the value of anger? What is the value of tolerance and compassion?

When those who do not consider afflictive emotions such as anger to be disadvantageous are distressed over an incident and get riled up, they feel they are perfectly right, even if they have a tiny bit of concern about how people might view them. Since they consider getting riled up to be normal, they make no effort to reduce anger. On the other hand, those who consider afflictive emotions to be negative and harmful do not voluntarily accept anger. Sometimes anger might win out and control them, but deep inside they do not happily receive it—there is some reluctance. Even if they do not take sufficient countermeasures, their inner reluctance about getting angry makes a great difference in the long run. Thus, it is important to reflect on the drawbacks of anger.

Use your good common sense. Is anger useful? If you get angry at someone, the result is good neither for you nor for the other person. Nothing helpful comes of it. In the end, anger does not harm others; it hurts yourself. When you are angry, good food is not tasty. When you are angry, even the faces of your spouse, children, or friends are irritating, not because their faces have changed but because something is wrong with your own attitude. When an unfortunate event happens, you can face and handle it more effectively without anger. Anger is almost useless. Perhaps a harsh word is needed sometimes to keep someone from a stupid deed, in the course of which anger may arise, but such anger should not be the primary motive; love and compassion should be. Actions stemming solely from anger are of no use at all; realizing this can serve to strengthen your determination to resist them.

It is not easy to have an intense bond of commiseration with each and every being, so do not be discouraged if a biased attitude interrupts your meditation. You will need the courage of unwavering effort throughout your life and for many lifetimes to come. Such a profound transformation cannot take place overnight, or in a week, or a month, or even a year. However, you will gradually notice changes in your reactions to individuals and the world. When old reactions creep back in, do not think this indicates the failure of meditation; rather, take such incidents as prods to meditate more.

BOOSTER IMAGINATION:
TAKING AND GIVING

When you see sentient beings troubled by suffering, it is good to know that their sufferings are due to their own actions (karma), and that you are therefore limited in how much you can help them directly. However, you can voluntarily and enthusiastically—from the depths of your heart—make the following wish and imagine with great force of will:

> This person is suffering very badly and, though wanting to gain happiness and alleviate suffering, does not know how to give up nonvirtues and adopt virtues. May his suffering as well as its causes ripen within me.

This is called the practice of taking others' suffering within using the instrument of compassion.

Correspondingly, from the depths of your heart you can wish and imagine that you give sufferers your happiness:

> I will give to these sentient beings without the slightest hesitation or regret whatever virtues I have accumulated in the form of good karma, which will be auspicious for them.

This is called the practice of giving away your own happiness within using the instrument of love.

Although such mental imagining does not actually bring about these results, it does increase determination and willpower, while creating a peaceful atmosphere. These practices are performed in conjunction with the inhalation and exhalation of the breath—inhaling others' pain, and exhaling your own happiness into their lives.

BOOSTER IMAGINATION:
USING MISFORTUNE

Similarly, when you are ill or suffer an unfortunate event, imagine:

> May this illness or misfortune serve as a substitute for the suffering of all sentient beings.

This will keep your suffering from getting worse through fretting about it, and it will enhance your courage. It is also helpful to think:

> May the suffering that I am undergoing now function as the ripening, manifestation, and conclusion of many bad karmas that I have accumulated.

In my limited experience, these practices really are sources of inner strength and will keep a smile on your face. Worry will not help, will it?

Recently, there was a rather strong earthquake in Dharmsala during my daily meditation on cultivating love and compassion. Though the earthquake was potentially life-threatening, I was not in the least afraid, which must have been due to being in the midst of reflecting on the needs of others. But I have to admit that just a couple of weeks ago, while flying for several hours through strong turbulence between Bombay and South Africa, I noticed that my palms were wet with sweat. So I reflected on the knowledge that if my karma meant that I had to die, then I simply had to die, and if not, the next morning I would be in South Africa. I felt better. The difference was in my outlook. If you can do something about a problem, do it; if it is impossible, worry is useless.

According to Tibetan Buddhist texts on training in altruism, when you are happy, do not get too excited about it, but dedicate to the welfare of all sentient beings the good karma that yields happiness; and when you suffer, take on yourself all sentient beings' pain. We usually have ups and downs, but in this way you can maintain inner courage, not allowing misfortune to disturb your peace of mind—neither too happy nor too sad, stable.

WHEN OTHERS TRY
TO TAKE ADVANTAGE
OF YOU

It may be that even if you remain a humble, honest, and contented person, some of your friends, neighbors, coworkers, or rivals will take advantage of you. To simply allow this is unreasonable. Under such circumstances, you must first clearly understand that the other person is a human being and has a right to be happy. With respect and compassion toward that person, you can act according to the circumstances she has created. This means responding strongly if necessary, but never losing your compassionate perspective. In fact, compassion is the only way to handle such a problem, since anger and irritation will only hinder effective action and complicate things. At first it is difficult to maintain compassion for someone who is being threatening or hurtful, but if you try again and again, you will find the way to react as strongly as the circumstances demand but without losing a loving attitude.

It is like the relation between a kind parent and children. Sometimes the child becomes stupid and naughty, and in order to stop that behavior, the father or mother acts—in accordance with those circumstances—with harsh words, perhaps even punishing the child, but without losing compassion. That is the way to handle the problem.

13

The Sixth Step:
Total Commitment

If one teaching is grasped and known, all of my teachings will be in the palm of your hand. What is this one
teaching? It is altruism.

—BUDDHA

What is the distinctive feature of *great* compassion? As
Kamalashila's *Stages of Meditation* says:

When you spontaneously feel compassion wishing
to completely eliminate the sufferings of all living
beings—just like a mother's wish to relieve her dear,
sweet child's sickness—then your compassion is complete and is therefore called great compassion.

Similarly, when from the depths of your heart you spontaneously feel love wishing to join all living beings with

true and lasting happiness, this is *great* love. For a mother whose dear child is suffering from sickness, no matter what she is doing, she—without any effort—has a keen sense of her child's problem, spontaneously wishing that the child be freed from that situation and be in a state of happiness. When you have such a profound, immediate sense of love and compassion for all beings, this is the measure of having generated great love and compassion.

Having cultivated the three levels of intensity of love and compassion and felt the full impact of those wishes, you are ready to practice the sixth step, the unusual altruism that calls for complete commitment on your part. This is the heartfelt decision in which you promise:

> Even if I have to do it alone, I will free all sentient beings from suffering and the causes of suffering, and join all sentient beings with happiness and its causes.

The willingness to take on the task alone is a heightened, special sense of altruism. Indeed, no one has to do this alone, but you are willing to do so if need be. In a decisive manner you are taking on full responsibility for others' well-being.

The causes favorable for assuming this burden are your previous cultivation of love and compassion; the favorable condition is realization of the fact that everyone has the Buddha nature, that the afflictive emotions in the minds of each and every being do not abide in the very nature of the mind but are removable. As I discussed earlier, problematic emotions can be separated from the mind, which means that enlightenment can be achieved.

Knowledge of these basic facts makes realistic the assumption of responsibility to help others on a vast scale. Since you understand that all afflicting obstructions can be removed, it is realistic to decide to help all beings do this. With these realizations you can make this altruistic decision from the depths of your heart and mind, which in turn opens the way for full spiritual development.

If you felt that some beings could not achieve enlightenment, this altruistic decision to help would be difficult. This is how wisdom works to assist in the development of love and compassion; seeing that suffering *can* be removed, you are moved from the depths about the plight of sentient beings, developing the determination to do something about it. If you could not do anything about it, such a decision would be impossible. For instance, I have made provision both here in Dharmsala and in Ladakh for a number of sheep not to be killed, but I cannot provide protected land for all sheep in these areas to wander freely. I can only be moved by mercy for the rest of them.

When you realize that there are techniques by which sentient beings can be protected from suffering, this stimulates a greater degree of proactive love and compassion. In this way, wisdom assists in your own decision to work to leave the round of cyclic pain and to help others do the same.

Meditation

Consider:

1. Distressing emotions do not dwell in the nature of the mind; therefore, they can be removed.

2. Since distressing emotions can be separated from the mind, it is realistic for me to work to achieve enlightenment and to help others do the same.

3. Resolve:
   Even if I have to do it alone, I will free all sentient beings from suffering and the causes of

suffering, and join all sentient beings with happiness and its causes.

Train in this until it becomes your natural motivation. This is true courage that can take you through all adversity.

14

The Seventh Step: Seeking Altruistic Enlightenment

The altruistic intention is to seek
Supreme enlightenment for the sake of others.

—MAITREYA, *ORNAMENT FOR CLEAR REALIZATION*

Once you generate the special altruistic attitude that you yourself must bring about the welfare of all beings by freeing them from suffering and connecting them with happiness, you must evaluate whether or not you have the capacity to accomplish this in your present state. Most likely you will decide that you do not. How, then, to proceed?

Helping others is not limited to providing food, shelter, and so forth but includes relieving the basic causes of suffering and providing the basic causes of happiness.

With respect to how to bring about such beneficence for others, it is the Buddhist view that one's own pleasure and pain are achieved by oneself and not generated from the outside and that, therefore, sentient beings themselves must understand and implement practices to bring about their own happiness. Just as in society, in addition to giving food, clothing, and shelter, we try to educate people so that they can take care of their own lives, so in the practice of altruism the most efficacious way to help others is through *teaching* what should be adopted in practice and what should be discarded from current behavior.

To teach this to others, first we must know their dispositions and interests and have full knowledge of beneficial practices. Therefore, it is necessary to achieve enlightenment in which the obstacles to realizing everything knowable are totally removed. This calls for fulfillment of your own potential to completely realize the nature of all persons and things and the removal of all obstacles to liberation from cyclic existence and full knowledge. This is the way you come to decide that, in order to bring about the welfare of others in a full way, it is necessary to attain enlightenment.

When you take on the basic outlook that, for the sake of all sentient beings, you seek to achieve enlightenment, you have attained an altruistic intention to become enlightened. Generation of this attitude is the last of the seven steps.

DECIDING TO ACHIEVE ENLIGHTENMENT

A strong altruistic attitude in which you promise to seek Buddhahood for the sake of others is built on the high-minded resolve of taking on yourself the burden of others' welfare. That, in turn, stems from compassion and love such that you cannot bear to see the manifest suffering of others or live with the knowledge that they are oppressed by unwanted internal conditions that result in suffering and limitation. Developing this sense of commiseration for others depends on seeing all sentient beings as close to you, like your best friend, and wanting to reciprocate their kindness. This itself stems from first seeing beings in an even-minded way. Therefore, for this final, seventh step you start by reviewing the previous steps.

Meditation

Based on your previous practice, you now can take all the previous steps to mind in a brief way with intense feeling.

Foundational Step: Equality

1. From their own point of view friends, enemies, and neutral beings equally want happiness and do not want suffering.

2. From your own point of view each and every one of them has been your friend limitless times over beginningless cyclic existence and will definitely help you again in the future; each has equally been your enemy; and each has equally been neutral.

3. Thus from whatever side it is considered, your own or others', there is no point in exaggerating feelings of intimacy or alienation. You should not value one person as basically good and another as bad, even though their present actions may be good or bad, helpful or harmful. There is no reason to be nice at heart to one person and not nice to another. Though it is true that people are friends or enemies temporarily—helpful or harmful—it is a mistake to use this fluid state as the basis for an inflexible attraction or hatred.

First Step: Recognizing Friends

1. Reflect that if there is rebirth, your births in cyclic existence have no beginning.

2. Consider that when you were born from a womb as an animal or human, or when you were born from an egg, you required a mother. Since your births are innumerable, you must have had innumerable mothers over the course of those many lifetimes. The implication is that every living being has been your mother at some time. If you have trouble coming to this conclusion, see whether you can find a reason why any sentient being has not been your mother; such a conclusion is impossible.

3. Draw the conclusion that the times you took birth from a womb or an egg are unlimited in number, and therefore your mothers are also unlimited in number.

4. Reflecting on these points, understand that each sentient being had to have been your mother many times. To do this:

- Bring to mind your best friend and identify that this friend was, at some time over the continuum of lives, a nurturing friend.

- Then gradually consider other, not so close friends one by one in the same way, identifying and feeling that over the continuum of lives, they were similarly close.

- Then bring to mind a neutral person—someone who has neither helped nor harmed you in this lifetime. Consider that this person was at certain times over the continuum of lives as close and as nurturing as your closest friend.

- Gradually extend this realization to other neutral persons—those seen on a subway, passed by on the street, or seen in a store.

- When you become somewhat proficient at identifying friends and neutral persons as having been nurturing friends and have felt how your perspective changes, consider a minor enemy—someone who has harmed you or your friends a little. Make sure to start with a minor enemy, so that you can develop experience with temporarily setting aside negative feelings to realize that at some time you were close friends.

- When you feel the change of perspective toward that minor enemy, stay with your new attitude for a while, and then slowly consider the next level of enemy.

Second Step: Appreciating Kindness

1. Visualize your mother, or prime nurturer, vividly in front of you.

2. Think:

   This person was my mother many times over the continuum of lives; in just this present lifetime she has bestowed on me a body that supports an auspicious life in which I am able to progress spiritually. She has sustained me in her womb for nine months, during which she could not behave as she wished but had to pay special attention to this burden that she carried in her body, making it heavy and difficult to move about. Even though my movements would cause her pain, she would take delight in them, thinking how strong her child was, rather than becoming angry and concentrating on her pain. Her sense of closeness and dearness was great. Stay a while with this thought, feeling its impact.

3. Deepen your appreciation by considering details: While giving birth, she suffered greatly, and afterward she was constantly concerned with my welfare, wondering how I was doing, valuing the child born from her own body higher than anything else. Later, she sustained me in the very best way she could.

   She wiped away my feces and removed mucus from my nose. She gave me her own milk and did not take offense when I bit her nipples. Even when she was bothered by such things, her sense of endearment for me was utmost in her mind. This was not just for a day, a week, a month, but from year to year, whereas for most people taking care of a child for an hour or two is bothersome.

   If you are using as your model a person other than your mother, recall in detail the kindnesses he or she extended to you.

4. Realize how dependent you were:

   > If she had abandoned me for even an hour or two, I could have died. Through her kindness in sustaining me with the best of food and clothing according to her ability, this precious life with a physical body that makes spiritual progress possible was maintained.

   Appreciate the kindness you received. When you carefully consider her kindness in these ways, there is no way not to be impressed.

5. Increase the scope of your appreciation to other lifetimes:

   > She was kind not only during this life, but also in other lifetimes as a human or as an animal, since most animals care for their young in similar ways.

   Let the impact of this new perspective sink in. Do not rush on to the next phase as if this were just a superficial exercise.

6. Having understood the kindness of your prime nurturer of this lifetime, extend this understanding gradually to other friends. When they were

your mother or best of friends, they protected you with great kindness just as your prime nurturer has done in this lifetime. Reflect slowly and carefully on their kindness, starting with your next closest friend and reflecting as above.

7. When the force of this reflection has been felt, pass to the next friend, meditating in the same manner, slowly considering all your friends, then neutral persons, and finally enemies.

Third Step: Returning Kindness

1. Think:

If my mother (or best friend) of this lifetime was blind and, not in her right mind, was proceeding along the edge of a frightful cliff without a guide, and if I, her own child, did not pay attention and take on the task of helping her, it would be awful.

2. Extend the example:

All sentient beings throughout space have been my mother and have protected me with great kindness; they do not know what in their behavior to discard and what to adopt in order to promote their own long-term interests. Without a spiritual guide, they are walking along the edge of a cliff of frightful sufferings in cyclic existence. If, knowing this, I did not consider their welfare but only my own freedom, it would be awful.

Stay a while with your perception of their perilous situation, feeling its impact. Allow yourself to care about everyone's situation. If this seems too vague, reflect on a specific person in this horrible situation, and then extend your intense feeling to everyone. Cultivating the earlier steps with regard to individual beings makes this possible.

3. In response to being cared for by others in this and other lifetimes, develop a determination to help them in whatever way is appropriate: "I will do whatever I can for these beings—my own nurturing friends—stricken by such suffering." Commit yourself to their welfare.

Fourth Step: Love

Part One

1. Bring to mind a friend and reflect on how this person suffers from mental and physical pain, from mistaking temporary pleasures for those that have an inner nature of happiness, and from being caught in a process outside of her control, just as you suffer in these ways.

2. Extend this reflection to more and more friends, one by one.

3. Apply this insight to several neutral persons, one by one.

4. Consider how the least of your enemies suffers in these ways, just as you do.

5. Slowly extend this to more and more of those who have harmed you or your friends.

Part Two

1. Notice that you naturally experience a sense of "I," as in "I want this," or "I do not want that."

2. Recognize that you naturally want happiness and do not want pain. This is both natural and correct, not requiring any further justification.

3. Based on this natural aspiration, you have the right to attain happiness and to get rid of suffering.

4. Just as you have these feelings and this right, so do others equally have the same feelings and the same right.

5. Reflect on the fact that the difference between yourself and others is that you are just one single person, whereas other beings are countless in number.

6. Pose this question: Should everyone be used for my attainment of happiness, or should I help others gain happiness?

7. Imagine yourself, calm and reasonable, looking to one side at another version of yourself—but this time selfish, overly proud, never thinking of others' welfare, concerned only with your own self, willing to do most anything to satisfy it.

8. On your other side imagine a number of destitute people unrelated to you, needy and in pain.

9. Now you—as an unbiased, sensible person in the middle—consider this: Both sides want happiness and want to get rid of pain; in this way, they are equal, the same. In addition, both have the right to accomplish these goals.

10. But think:

> The selfishly motivated person on one side is only a single person, whereas the others are far greater in number, even limitless. Is this single self-centered person more important? Or is the group of poor, needy, helpless people more important?

> Which side will you join? You, as the unbiased person in the middle, will naturally favor the greater number of suffering people; there is no way to avoid the overwhelming needs of the greater number, especially in contrast to that proud and foolish character. If you have a warm heart, you will be drawn naturally to the side of the needy beings.

11. Reflect:

> If I, as just one person, take advantage of the majority, I am acting contrary to my humanity. Indeed, to sacrifice one hundred dollars for the sake of one dollar is very foolish; to spend one dollar for the sake of one hundred dollars is smart.

12. Thinking this way, decide:

> I am going to place my emphasis on the many rather than on this one selfish person.

Just as every part of your body is equally considered to be your body and therefore to be equally protected from pain, so all sentient beings should be equally protected from suffering.

Part Three

1. Starting with your best friend, think:

> This person wants happiness but is bereft. How nice it would be if he could be imbued with happiness and all the causes of happiness!

Meditate this way over a long period of time until you generate a sense of cherishing your best friend like a mother does her sweet, beloved child. Though this is easy to do with respect to such a good friend, take your time. Notice your feelings; they will be a model to extend to others.

2. Continue the same meditation with respect to more and more friends until this wish for happiness and all the causes of happiness is equally strong for all of them. Do this one by one:

> This person wants happiness but is bereft. How nice it would be if she could be imbued with happiness and all the causes of happiness!

If your feeling is not as strong as it is for your best friend, renew the feeling of the earlier steps, reflecting on their wanting happiness and not wanting suffering, their having been your best friend in the course of cyclic existence, their having been kind to you, and their deserving reciprocation of that kindness.

3. Imagining a neutral being in front of you, think:

> This person wants happiness but is bereft. How nice it would be if he could be imbued with happiness and all the causes of happiness!

Make sure not to let the meditation turn into just words; the point is to alter your perspective based on your feelings for your best friend.

4. Continue the same meditation with respect to more and more neutral persons until this wish for happiness and all the causes of happiness is equally strong for friends and neutral persons.

5. Imagining your least of enemies in front of you, contemplate:

    This person wants happiness but is bereft. How nice it would be if she could be imbued with happiness and all the causes of happiness!

    Stay with this practice until you actually feel the heartfelt wish for happiness and all the causes of happiness for this person who has harmed you or your friends. Keep this up until it is as strong as it is for friends and neutral persons.

6. Continue the same practice with respect to another enemy, such as someone who has bothered you at work or in public. As you succeed, slowly consider more and more enemies, gradually widening the scope of your sense of love.

Part Four

1. Starting with your best friend, think:

    This person wants happiness but is bereft. May he be imbued with happiness and all the causes of happiness!

2. Extend the same wish to more and more friends, to the point where the call for happiness and all the causes of happiness is equally strong for all of them.

    This person wants happiness but is bereft. May she be imbued with happiness and all the causes of happiness!

3. Imagining a neutral being in front of you, think as follows:

    This person wants happiness but is bereft. May he be imbued with happiness and all the causes of happiness!

4. Continue the same meditation with respect to more and more neutral persons until the call for happiness and all the causes of happiness is equally strong for friends and neutral persons.

5. Imagine the least of your enemies in front of you, and contemplate:

> This person wants happiness but is bereft. May he be imbued with happiness and all the causes of happiness!

Reflect on this until you experience the heartfelt call for happiness and all the causes of happiness for this person who has harmed you or your friends. Do so until it is as strong as it is for friends and neutral persons. This takes time.

6. Continue the same practice with respect to another enemy, such as someone who has irritated you and made you upset:

> This person wants happiness but is bereft. May she be imbued with happiness and all the causes of happiness!

Only when your feeling is strong and sincere, consider another enemy, and then another, gradually widening the circle of your love.

Part Five

1. Starting with your best friend, think:

    I will do whatever I can to cause him to be imbued with happiness and all the causes of happiness!

    Notice the strength of your feeling of involvement.

2. Extend the same intention to more and more friends to the point where your commitment to their attaining happiness and all the causes of happiness is equally strong for all of them.

    I will do whatever I can to cause her to be imbued with happiness and all the causes of happiness!

3. Imagining a neutral being in front of you, think as forcefully as you can:

    I will do whatever I can to cause him to be imbued with happiness and all the causes of happiness!

4. Continue the same meditation with respect to more and more neutral persons until your involvement in

their attaining happiness and all the causes of happiness is equally strong for friends and neutral persons.

5. Imagining your least of enemies in front of you, contemplate:

> I will do whatever I can to cause her to be imbued with happiness and all the causes of happiness!

Use various reflections based on the earlier steps until you experience—as strongly as you do for friends and neutral persons—the same deep involvement in the attainment of happiness and all the causes of happiness by this person who has harmed you or your friends. This takes time.

6. Continue the same practice with respect to another enemy, such as someone who has irritated you and made you upset:

> I will do whatever I can to cause him to be imbued with happiness and all the causes of happiness!

Only when your feeling is strong and sincere, consider another enemy, and then another, gradually widening the circle of your committed love.

Fifth Step: Compassion

Part One

1. Bring to mind a friend who has obvious pain, and think:

> Like me, this person wants happiness and does not want suffering, yet is stricken with such pain. If this person could only be free from suffering and the causes of suffering!

Analyze the ways this person suffers until you have a strong feeling of how wonderful it would be if she could be free from pain of all sorts, and then stay with that feeling, letting go of the analysis. Then, when the feeling diminishes, analyze how the person suffers, and when you feel strong commiseration and a wish for her relief, stick with it without analysis. This is called alternating analytic meditation and stabilizing meditation. Perform the two back and forth so that the intensity of feeling remains strong. Eventually, the two types of meditation will assist and further each other without your having to switch between them.

2. Visualize before you a friend who, even though not blatantly suffering, will suffer in the future due to substantial counterproductive actions of the kind that we all have committed over the course of beginningless time. Think:

> Like me, this person wants happiness and does not want suffering, yet is stricken with such pain. If this person could only be free from suffering and the causes of suffering!

Alternate analytic and stabilizing meditation.

3. Slowly extend this meditation person by person, first with more friends, then with neutral persons, and finally with enemies, eventually including all sentient beings throughout space.

Part Two

1. Bring to mind a friend who suffers obvious pain, and think:

> Like me, this person wants happiness and does not want suffering, yet is stricken with such pain. May this person only be free from the suffering and the causes of suffering!

Alternate analytic and stabilizing meditation.

2. Visualize in front of you a friend who, even though not blatantly suffering, will suffer in the future due to substantial counterproductive actions of the kind that we all have committed over the course of beginningless time. Think:

> Like me, this person wants happiness and does not want suffering, yet is stricken with such pain. May this person only be free from the suffering and the causes of suffering!

Alternate analytic and stabilizing meditation.

3. Slowly extend this meditation person by person, first with more friends, then with neutral persons, and finally with enemies, eventually including all sentient beings throughout space.

Part Three

1. Bring to mind a friend who has obvious pain, and think:

> Like me, this person wants happiness and does not want suffering, yet is stricken with such pain. I will help this person be free from suffering and all the causes of suffering!

Alternate analytic and stabilizing meditation.

2. Visualize in front of you a friend who, even though not stricken with blatant suffering, will suffer in the future due to substantial counter-productive actions of the kind that we all have committed over the course of beginningless time. Think:

> Like me, this person wants happiness and does not want suffering, yet is stricken with such pain. I will help this person be free from suffering and all the causes of suffering!

Alternate analytic and stabilizing meditation.

3. Slowly extend this meditation person by person, first with more friends, then with neutral persons, and finally with enemies, eventually including all sentient beings throughout space.

Sixth Step: Total Commitment

1. Distressing emotions do not dwell in the nature of the mind; therefore, they can be removed.

2. Since distressing emotions can be separated from the mind, it is realistic for me to work to achieve enlightenment and to help others do the same.

3. Even if I have to do it alone, I will free all sentient beings from suffering and the causes of suffering, and join all sentient beings with happiness and its causes.

Seventh Step: Seeking Altruistic Enlightenment

Having reviewed the previous meditations, you are ready for the final step, deciding to achieve enlightenment for the sake of helping others.

1. Analyze whether in your present state you have the capacity to bring about the welfare of all beings by freeing them from suffering and joining them with happiness.

2. Consider that in addition to giving food, clothing, and shelter, it is necessary to educate people so that they can take care of their own lives. *Teaching* what should be adopted and discarded is crucial, and therefore we must know their dispositions and interests and have full knowledge of beneficial practices.

3. Realize that though you can help others on a limited level, you cannot yet do so on a vast level.

4. Conclude that thus it is necessary to achieve enlightenment, in which the obstacles keeping you from realizing everything knowable are completely removed and you gain total realization of the nature of persons and things.

5. Decide that in order to bring about the welfare of others in a full way, you will achieve enlightenment.

As your activities of body, speech, and mind become more and more directed to the benefit of others, you develop a profound sense of love and commitment.

15

The Enormous Power
of Altruism

Is there any virtue equal to this altruistic intention?
Is there any such friend?

—SHANTIDEVA, *A GUIDE TO THE BODHISATTVA WAY OF LIFE*

Just as the five elements of the physical environment—
space, earth, water, fire, and wind—are without limit, so
the sentient beings that the altruistic person seeks to lead
out of suffering to the state of enlightenment are limitless
in number. Bodhisattvas' strength of heart is such that
they are committed to this task of relieving all beings—
without any limitation of friend or foe, nationality or eth-
nic group—from each and every type of suffering. They
want to establish them in a state of enlightenment endowed with all possible favorable qualities. To become
able to help on such a vast scale, they are willing—from

the depths of their hearts—to train in innumerable techniques to advance toward their own perfection no matter how long it takes, over eons and eons, with effort that is like invisible armor, preventing impatience and discouragement. Since their perspective is so vast, they accrue meritorious positive karma even when they are sleeping, power as limitless as the limitless beings to whom they have dedicated themselves.

When you consider the vast power of enlightenment and the huge amount of meritorious practice needed to attain it, you might become discouraged and shrink from the task. However, since the sentient beings who are the recipients of your love and compassion are limitless in number, the beneficial forces accumulated by your altruistic mind are also limitless. In this way, the limitless qualities of enlightenment, which might seem hard to achieve due to their vastness, can be seen as attainable. Reflecting this way, you see that transformation into enlightenment is indeed possible, thereby preventing any possibility of laziness and procrastination.

As Nagarjuna's *Precious Garland of Advice* says:

Through their love and compassion
The altruistic are determined to lead

Limitless sentient beings out of suffering
And establish them in Buddhahood.

Hence even when sleeping,
After thoroughly assuming such resolve
Those who remain steadfast—
Even though they might not be meticulous—

Always accumulate merit as limitless as all
    sentient beings
Since sentient beings are limitless.
Know then that because the causes are limitless,
Limitless Buddhahood is not hard to attain.

The altruistic stay for a limitless time in the
    world;
For limitless beings they seek
The limitless qualities of enlightenment
And perform limitless virtuous actions.

Hence though enlightenment is limitless,
How could they not attain it
With these four limitless factors
Without taking too long!

By aiming the scope of your actions not just at yourself or a few close persons, but at each and every being throughout space, the transformative effect of your positive actions is multiplied by the limitless number of beings who are the field of your intent. In this way, love becomes the indispensable ingredient and cause of full enlightenment. Though at first you might question the possibility of Buddhahood, full spiritual transformation becomes realistic when you consider the effectiveness of love, compassion, and the altruistic intention to become enlightened. They will support you on your spiritual path, and you will be amazed at their power.

BOOSTER WISHES

Heartfelt wishes for your own future spiritual development and for the progress of others is itself a form of meditation. Nagarjuna, famed in India and throughout Asia for identifying exaggerated perceptions of the nature of persons and things and for his presentation of the relation of cause and effect, composed a set of marvelous wishes for your own and others' prosperity in terms of personal health, resources, and spiritual qualities. Here they are:

Through the merit of virtuous deeds
That I did earlier and will do
May all sentient beings aspire
To the highest enlightenment.

May all sentient beings have stainless faculties,
Release from all conditions of oppression,
Freedom of action,
And endowment with good livelihood.

Also may all sentient beings
Have jewels in their hands,
And may all the limitless necessities of life remain
Unconsumed as long as there is cyclic existence.

May all persons at all times
Be born in advantageous ways.
May all sentient beings have
The intelligence of wisdom and the legs of morality.

May sentient beings have a pleasant complexion,
Good physique, great splendor,
A pleasing appearance, freedom from disease,
Strength, and long life.

May all be skilled in the means to extinguish
    suffering
And have liberation from all pain,
Inclination to spiritual practice,
And the great wealth of spiritual teachings.

May they be adorned with love, compassion,
    joy,
Even-mindedness devoid of afflictive emotions,
Giving, morality, patience, effort,
Concentration, and wisdom.

Completing the two collections of merit and
    wisdom,
May they physically have brilliant marks and
    beautiful features,
And may they cross without interruption
The full range of spiritual development.

May I also be adorned completely
With those and all other good qualities,
Be freed from all defects,
And have superior love for all sentient beings.

May I perfect all the virtues
For which all sentient beings hope,
And may I always relieve
The sufferings of all embodied beings.

May those beings in all worlds
Who are distressed through fear
Become entirely fearless
Even through merely hearing my name.

Through seeing or thinking of me or only hearing
    my name
May beings attain great joy,
Naturalness free from error,
Definiteness toward complete enlightenment,

And the five clairvoyances
Throughout their continuum of lives.
May I always in all ways bring
Help and happiness to all sentient beings.

May I always without harm
Simultaneously stop
All beings in all worlds
Who wish to commit ill deeds.

May I always be an object of enjoyment
For all sentient beings according to their wish
And without interference, as are the earth,
Water, fire, wind, herbs, and wild forests.

May I be as dear to sentient beings as their own life,
And may they be even more dear to me.
May their ill deeds fructify for me,
And all my virtues fructify for them.

As long as any sentient being
Anywhere has not been liberated,
May I remain in the world for the sake of that being
Though I have attained highest enlightenment.

Nagarjuna then speaks about the value of taking these wishes to heart:

If the merit of saying this
Had form, it would never fit
Into realms of worlds as numerous
As the sand grains of the Ganges River.

The enlightened said so,
And the reasoning is this:
The limitlessness of the merit of wishing to help
    limitless realms
Of sentient beings is like the limitlessness of those
    beings.

By truly taking these wishes to heart, you dedicate your deepest aims to the well-being of others, thereby accumulating positive forces as great as the count of sentient beings who comprise your field of altruistic intention.

16

Acting with Love

Without hope of reward
Provide help to others.

—NAGARJUNA, *PRECIOUS GARLAND OF ADVICE*

With altruistic motivation every action accumulates virtues—the limitless power of salutary merit. About giving, or charity, Nagarjuna's *Friendly Letter* says:

There is no better friend for the future
Than giving—bestowing gifts properly
On monastics, clergy, the poor, and friends—
Knowing resources to be evanescent and pithless.

Giving with altruism means to train from the depths of the heart in an attitude of generosity such that you are not seeking any reward or result for yourself. Think of the act of charity and all of its beneficial results as aimed solely toward the benefit of others. Even though charity can be performed by those seeking their own benefit, such as when someone makes a charitable donation in order to become famous, altruistic giving involves no selfishness at all. Therefore its effects, both for yourself and for others, are far greater than they otherwise could be. In this way, generosity is like a friend for yourself and for others in the future.

From your own point of view, the impermanence of this present life will force you to leave all wealth behind, but by giving it away, you can take it with you as good karma. As Nagarjuna's *Precious Garland* says,

> You are living amidst the causes of death
> Like a lamp standing in a breeze.
> Having let go of all possessions,
> At death powerless you must go elsewhere,
> But all that has been used for spiritual practice
> Will precede you as good karma.

If you use it for beneficial purposes, the resultant good karma is carried to the next lifetime, but if you hold on to it with attachment, that itself will keep wealth away from you in future lives:

> If you do not make contributions of the wealth
> Obtained from former giving to the needy,
> Through your ingratitude and attachment
> You will not obtain resources in the future.

Those to whom you make donations are like workers carrying good karma to your future lives:

> Here in the world workers do not carry
> Provisions for a journey unpaid,
> But lowly beggars, without being bribed, carry to
>   your future life
> What you give them multiplied a hundred times.

In this way, generosity also helps you in that it yields resources for use during future lives.

Therefore, in just the way that you focus on furthering your own interests, dedicate yourself to helping others:

Just as you are intent on thinking
Of what could be done to help yourself,
So you should be intent on thinking
Of what could be done to help others.

Make yourself available for others like a natural resource:

If only for a moment make yourself
Available for the use of others
Just as earth, water, fire, wind, medicine,
And parks are available to all.

Analyze each situation to determine what will help. Even
poison is known to counteract certain problems:

Even give poison
To those whom it will help,
But do not give even the best food
To those whom it will not help.
The Buddha said that if it helps others,
You should even bring temporary discomfort.

LOVE AND POLITICS

Love and compassion should be the basis of politics. They make a politician beloved without requiring that he or she be weak.

Leaders whose nature is generosity
Are liked if they are strong,
Like a sweet hardened outside
With cardamom and pepper.

The birds of the populace will alight upon
The royal tree providing the shade of patience,
Flourishing flowers of respect,
And large fruits of resplendent giving.

The message is that politicians should always be expansive of heart:

Always be of exalted mind
And take delight in exalted deeds.
From exalted actions arise
All effects that are exalted.

Nagarjuna calls on political leaders to provide many types of public assistance:

> Always care compassionately
> For the sick, the unprotected, those stricken
> With suffering, the lowly, and the poor
> And take special care to nourish them.

> Provide extensive care
> For the persecuted, the victims of crop failure,
> The stricken, those suffering contagion,
> And for beings in conquered areas.

> Cause the blind, the sick, the lowly,
> The protectorless, the destitute,
> And the crippled equally to obtain
> Food and drink without interruption.

> In order to alleviate the suffering
> Of sentient beings—old, young, and infirm—
> You should establish through the resources that
>   you control
> Doctors and health workers throughout your
>   country.

Lovingly give to beggars
Various and glittering clothes,
Adornments, perfumes,
Garlands, and enjoyments.

Prisoners are to be treated with love, even when punished:

Just as deficient children are punished
Out of a wish to make them competent,
So punishment should be carried out with
    compassion,
Not through hatred nor desire for wealth.

Even to those whom they have rightfully
    fined,
Bound, punished, and so forth,
You, being moistened with compassion,
Should always be caring.

Through compassion you should
Always generate just an attitude of altruism
Even for those persons
Who have committed awful ill deeds.

Especially generate compassion
For those whose ill deeds are horrible, the
    murderers.
Those of fallen nature are receptacles
Of compassion from those whose nature is
    magnanimous.

Free the weaker prisoners
After a day or five days.
Do not think the others
Are not to be freed under any conditions.

As long as prisoners are not freed,
They should be made comfortable
With barbers, baths, food, drink,
Medicine, and clothing.

Once you have analyzed and thoroughly
    recognized
The angry murderers,
Have them banished
Without killing or tormenting them.

Providing schools is particularly important:

As ways to increase wisdom,
Wherever there is a school in the land
Provide for the livelihood of teachers
And give lands to them for their provision.

TYPES OF GIVING

In these ways "giving" refers to an attitude of generosity as well as those physical and verbal acts motivated by generosity. Altruistic giving requires forsaking all miserliness, being solely concerned with relieving another's poverty, and not being concerned about getting anything out of it for yourself. If you sought profit for yourself from an act of charity in the future, it would be like giving a loan with interest. Rather, dedicate it only to others, instead of looking forward to the favorable karmic results that will indeed accrue to you. Practicing generosity calls for developing a willingness to give away all possessions.

Giving is of three types:

1. Donating material things such as money, clothing, and food; making gifts to the poor and the sick, and donations for education and the provision of medical care;

2. Providing clear teachings about spiritual practices as well as about proper types of worldly livelihood, such as in becoming a medical practitioner, and giving encouragement to undertake moral behavior;

3. Giving relief from fearful situations by protecting beings from robbers, unjust governments, ferocious animals, flood, fire, and so forth. This includes protecting animals; even help a bug out of a puddle.

Though difficult, it is important to imagine giving away your own good karmas, which are like roots giving rise to favorable circumstances in the future. By having a strong sense of dedicating your roots of virtue to others, you will no longer seek for any reward for yourself. The reward, thereby, will be greater than you could imagine.

Meditation

1. Imagine many destitute beings, impoverished in various ways, in front of yourself.

2. Imagine the many types of food, clothing, shelter, and so forth that those beings need, and give these to them.

If you enact this technique again and again, your mind will become deeply imbued with an attitude of generosity.

MY FINAL ADVICE

Love and compassion are most important, most precious, most powerful, and most sacred. Practicing them is useful not only in terms of true religion but also in worldly life for both mental and physical health. They are the basic elements supporting our life and happiness. With practice they become effective and beneficial driving forces for life.

Selected Readings

H. H. the Dalai Lama, Tenzin Gyatso. *How to Practice: The Way to a Meaningful Life.* Translated and edited by Jeffrey Hopkins. New York: Atria Books/Simon & Schuster, 2002.

———. *Kindness, Clarity, and Insight.* Translated and edited by Jeffrey Hopkins; coedited by Elizabeth Napper. Ithaca, N.Y.: Snow Lion, 1984.

———. *The Meaning of Life: Buddhist Perspectives on Cause and Effect.* Translated and edited by Jeffrey Hopkins. Boston: Wisdom, 2000.

———. *Mind of Clear Light: Advice on Living Well and Dying Consciously.* Translated and edited by Jeffrey Hopkins. New York: Atria Books/Simon & Schuster, 2002.

Hopkins, Jeffrey. *Buddhist Advice for Living and Liberation: Nagarjuna's "Precious Garland."* Ithaca, N.Y.: Snow Lion, 1998.

———. *Cultivating Compassion.* New York: Broadway Books, 2001.

Lekden, Kensur. *Meditations of a Tibetan Tantric Abbot.* Translated and edited by Jeffrey Hopkins. Ithaca, N.Y.: Snow Lion, 2001.

Rinchen, Geshe Sonam, and Ruth Sonam. *Yogic Deeds of Bodhisattvas: Gyel-tsap on Aryadeva's Four Hundred.* Ithaca, N.Y.: Snow Lion, 1994.

Tsongkhapa. *The Great Treatise on the Stages of the Path to Enlightenment.* Vols. 1–3. Translated and edited by Joshua W. C. Cutler and Guy Newland. Ithaca, N.Y.: Snow Lion, 2000–2004.

Wallace, Vesna A., and B. Alan Wallace. *A Guide to the Bodhisattva Way of Life.* Ithaca, N.Y.: Snow Lion, 1997.